Letts

rev Go

Steve Cushing

ICT

Contents

This book and your GCSE course   4

Preparing for the examination   7

Using search engines   8

1 Information systems   9

1.1 Introduction   9

1.2 Inputs, processing and outputs   10

1.3 Data within information systems   11

Sample GCSE questions   15

Exam practice questions   15

2 Hardware   16

2.1 Main components of a computer system   16

2.2 Input peripherals, or devices   19

2.3 Output peripherals, or devices   29

2.4 Storage devices and media   35

Sample GCSE questions   43

Exam practice questions   44

3 Software   46

3.1 Operating environment and systems tasks   46

3.2 Communicating with the operating system   51

3.3 Applications software   53

Sample GCSE questions   73

Exam practice questions   76

4 Networks and the Internet   82

4.1 Networks and communications   82

4.2 Computer to computer communication   84

4.3 External communications links   91

4.4 What is the Internet?   94

4.5 Email   100

4.6 Entering data   102

Sample GCSE questions   104

Exam practice questions   107

5 Designing systems   109

5.1 Systems and applications   109

Sample GCSE questions   118

Exam practice questions   120

6 Security   121

6.1 Security of systems and data   121

6.2 Passwords, encryption and back-ups   126

6.3 Data quality   128

6.4 Misuse of data   133

Sample GCSE questions   137

Exam practice questions   138

7 Information systems in society   139

7.1 ICT in commerce and at work   141

7.2 Mail-order company   142

Sample GCSE questions   146

Exam practice questions   147

8 Health and safety   148

8.1 Health and safety   148

Sample GCSE questions   152

Exam practice questions   153

Exam practice answers   154

Mock examination paper   159

Index   175

This book and your GCSE course

Use these pages to get to know your course.
- Make sure you know your examination board
- Make sure that you have completed all the necessary work
- Make sure that you know how many examination papers you have to take.

	AQA A	AQA B	Edexcel	OCR A	OCR B	WJEC	NICCEA	Key Skills
1.1 Introduction								
1.2 Inputs, processing and outputs	✓	✓	✓	✓	✓	✓	✓	
1.3 Data within information systems	✓	✓	✓	✓	✓	✓	✓	
2.1 Main components of a computer system	✓	✓	✓	✓	✓	✓	✓	
2.2 Input peripherals, or devices	✓	✓	✓	✓	✓	✓	✓	
2.3 Output peripherals, or devices	✓	✓	✓	✓	✓	✓	✓	
2.4 Storage devices and media	✓	✓	✓	✓	✓	✓	✓	
3.1 Operating environment and systems tasks	✓	✓	✓	✓	✓	✓	✓	
3.2 Communicating with the operating system	✓	✓	✓	✓	✓	✓	✓	
3.3 Applications software	✓	✓	✓	✓	✓	✓	✓	✓
4.1 Networks and communications	✓	✓	✓	✓		✓	✓	
4.2 Computer to computer communication	✓	✓	✓	✓	✓	✓	✓	
4.3 External communications links	✓	✓	✓	✓	✓	✓	✓	✓
4.4 What is the Internet?	✓	✓	✓	✓	✓	✓	✓	✓
4.5 Email	✓	✓	✓	✓	✓	✓	✓	✓
4.6 Entering data	✓	✓	✓	✓	✓	✓	✓	✓
5.1 Systems and applications	✓	✓	✓	✓	✓	✓	✓	
6.2 Passwords, encryption and backups	✓	✓	✓	✓	✓	✓	✓	✓
6.3 Data quality	✓	✓	✓	✓	✓	✓	✓	✓
6.4 Misuse of data	✓	✓	✓	✓	✓	✓	✓	✓
7.1 Introduction	✓	✓	✓	✓	✓	✓	✓	✓
7.2 Mail-order company	✓	✓	✓	✓		✓		
8.1 Health and safety	✓	✓	✓	✓	✓	✓	✓	✓

Visit your awarding body website for full details of your course or download your complete GCSE specification.

AQA A

AQA A GCSE consists of **one written examination** paper that is taken by full course candidates. This consists of **1½ hours** of **short answer questions for Foundation** tier and **2 hours** of **short and extended answer questions for Higher tier** candidates. All questions are compulsory and relate to general ICT use. You will need to understand all the relevant sections of this revision guide for this examination paper.

AQA B

AQA B GCSE consists of **one written examination** paper that is taken by full course candidates. This consists of **1½ hours** of **short answer questions for Foundation** tier and **2 hours** of **short and extended answer questions for Higher** tier candidates. All questions are compulsory and some require longer written responses. All are set in contexts, for example home, school, recreation, community, business and industry. In these contexts, you are given opportunities to acquire competence, capability and critical skills through the creation, implementation, use and evaluation of a range of ICT systems. You will need to understand relevant sections of this book as applied to the case study.

OCR A

OCR A GCSE consists of **two examination papers for the full course**, and **one examination paper for the short course**. The first examination paper for the full course is the same as the examination paper for the short course. Paper one tests knowledge and understanding of computer systems, communications technology and information management. In two tiers, **Foundation 1 hour** and **Higher 1¼ hours**, the questions mainly require short responses, single word answers or one or two sentences, although you are required to give extended responses to questions targeted at the higher grades. The second paper, also in two tiers, **Foundation 1 hour** and **Higher 1¼ hours**, tests knowledge and understanding of ICT applications, systems, networks and computer technology and the theoretical aspects of problem solving. You will need to understand all the relevant sections of this revision guide for both examination papers.

OCR B

OCR B GCSE consists of **two examination papers for the full course**, and **one examination paper for the short course**. The first examination paper for the full course is the same as the examination paper for the short course. This examination paper is a Key Skill test at level one or two and lasts one hour. It consists of multiple-choice questions based upon developing information, presenting information and searching for information. Paper two of the full course is based upon a set context issued in advance, and you will be expected to demonstrate your knowledge through this specific set context. The paper is in two tiers, **Foundation 1 hour** and **Higher 1½ hours**. All candidates will need to understand the sections related to Key Skills for paper one. If you are a full course candidate will need to understand relevant sections of this book as applied to the specified case study for paper two.

Edexcel

Edexcel GCSE consists of **one two-hour examination** paper that is taken by both short and full course candidates. The paper is divided into three sections A, B and C. Full course candidates sit all **three** sections and short course candidates leave the examination room after one hour, completing sections **A and B only**. All questions are compulsory. Section A is multiple choice, with questions based upon your ICT knowledge. Section B is based upon a set case study. The compulsory questions require you to complete a selection of design tasks relating to the set problem. In addition, you may be asked questions that relate to aspects of the implementation and testing of a solution to the stated problem. Section C requires general ICT knowledge. You will need to understand all the relevant sections of this revision guide for sections A and C and sections relevant to the case study for section B.

WJEC

WJEC GCSE consists of **two examination papers for the full course**, and **one examination paper for the short course**. The first examination paper for the full course is the same as the examination paper for the short course. Paper one covers the requirements of Information Technology at Key Stage 4 in the National Curriculum and also the external test in the Key Skill of Information Technology. It specifically assesses IT – use and impact on society. The paper is in two tiers, **Foundation 1 hour** and **Higher 1½ hours**. Paper two assesses IT applications. This paper is also in two tiers, **Foundation 1 hour** and **Higher 1½ hours**. You will need to understand all the relevant sections of this revision guide for both examination papers.

NICCEA/ICAA

NICCEA/ICAA GCSE consists of **two examination papers for the full course**, and **one examination paper for the short course**. The first examination paper for the full course is the same as the examination paper for the short course. This examination paper is a Key Skill test and consists of multiple choice questions based upon developing information, presenting information and searching for information. Paper two of the full course covers general ICT applications. The paper is in two tiers, **Foundation 1 hour** and **Higher 1½ hours**. All candidates will need to understand the sections related to Key Skills for paper one. If you are a full course candidate you will need to understand all the relevant sections of this revision guide for paper two.

Preparing for the examination

Success in GCSE examinations comes from an organised approach throughout the subject course and a positive attitude to the examination, or examinations, that terminate it. The following approach may help you throughout your ICT GCSE course.

Know your course

Check which examination you are taking and see which sections of this book you need to study. Some examinations focus upon a context, for example using ICT in the health service. Others require you to demonstrate your knowledge through general ICT use.

Planning your study

- After completing a topic in school or college, go through it again in this revision guide.
- Try copying out the main points, or use a highlighter pen to emphasise them. A couple of days later, try to write out these key points from memory.
- Check any differences between what you wrote or highlighted originally, and what you wrote later.
- Keep any notes that you write for revision before the examination.
- Try some questions in the book and check the answers.
- Decide whether you feel confident about the topic, noting any weaknesses that you feel you have. If possible, discuss these with your teacher/tutor.

Preparing a revision programme

- When you start to revise for the examination (you should allow yourself a number of weeks), check through the list of topics in your Examination Board's specification.
- Identify topics that you are not confident about. You should spend time on these topics, rather than spending valuable revision time on things you already know and can do.
- When you feel that you have mastered a section, try past questions on it. Always check the answers carefully.
- In the final fortnight before the examination, go back to your original note sheets, or highlighting in this guide.

Exam technique

You will have a more positive attitude to the examination if you feel you have prepared for it properly. A good examination technique will also improve your performance. Remember the following basics:

- Read the instructions on the front of the examination paper carefully to make sure you know how many questions to attempt.
- Read the questions very carefully, paying particular attention to words of instruction such as State or Describe or Explain or Show or List or Compare.
- Carefully note the time available to complete the examination. Aim to divide up your time before you start. For example, if an examination is two hours long and contains eight questions that you should attempt, allow yourself about fifteen minutes for each question if each of the questions gives you roughly the same number of marks. You should aim to attempt all questions rather than spending all your time on a few.
- Examination papers usually tell you how many marks are available for each answer. The number of marks gives you a guide to the importance of the question and often to the amount you ought to write.
- Check before the end of the examination that you have not missed out any pages. Remember to turn over the last page, too.
- Try to leave time to check your work through carefully.

Using search engines

Although people refer to all search devices on the web as search engines there are two types of systems in use. AltaVista and Infoseek are **search engines**, while Yahoo is a **directory**. Search engines employ specialised software to scan the Web and store information in gigantic databases. When you use a search engine you do not search the web, you search the directory.

Knowing what to ask for

To use search engines effectively, you need to think of **search terms** or **key words**. Effective searches on the Internet use words and language that are **universal**. Some of the better search engines allow you to tell them what you do not want, as well as what you do. This is usually achieved by placing a − (minus) sign in front of of the words you do not want.

Common symbols for using search engines effectively

If you type in the key words *broken legs*, a search engine will search for all documents that contain *broken* and/or *legs*, giving highest priority to those that contain both words. This could result in a long and confusing list of possible contacts.

If only lower case letters are used, the search will find documents that contain the words regardless of whether they are in lower or upper case. If a mixture of upper and lower case is specified, the search will try to find words that match the words exactly, e.g. Broken Legs.

Advanced searches

Search engines have slightly different requirements for carrying out advanced searches. The general rules are as follows.

+ and −

- If you put a + in front of a word, documents will be found that contain that word, e.g. +broken+legs will find all documents that contain the word broken and also the word legs; broken+legs would give a list of documents that contain the word legs but will not necessarily be about being broken.
- If you put a − in front of a word, documents will be found that don't contain that word, e.g. +broken−legs would give a list of documents that contain the word broken but miss out those that contain legs.

AND, OR, AND NOT

The word **AND** can be used to combine **key words**. All words joined by AND must be contained in the document for it to be listed in the results of a search.

OR can be used to **combine** key words. At least one of the words joined by OR must be contained in the document for it to be listed in the results of the search. OR is often used to link words that have a similar meaning in a search, for example jam OR marmalade.

AND NOT is also used to combine key words. The search will not include documents containing the word AND NOT. For example AND NOT marmalade would produce documents relating to jam, but not any containing the word marmalade.

Brackets

Brackets can group words together to make a more complex search possible, e.g. horses AND (dogs OR cats) would produce a list of documents containing the word horses and either the word dogs, or cats, or both.

Wild card

The character * is called a wild card and can be used to stand for any character or set of characters. For example, typing auto* would produce a list of documents containing words such as automobile, automatic, autogiro, autopsy, and so on.

Titles

A search can be limited to the titles of documents or websites. If the words are important to the document or website, they may well be contained in the title. The search engine is instructed to do this by typing t: before the key word(s). For example,
t: "fuel shortage" would search titles containing those words, in that order.

1 Information systems

The following topics are covered in this chapter:

- 1.1 Introduction
- 1.2 Inputs, processing and outputs
- 1.3 Data within information systems

1.1 Introduction

Description of information systems

OCR A OCR B
EDEXCEL
AQA A AQA B
NICCEA
WJEC

Initially computers were developed as a standalone technology designed to perform specific functions such as sequences of calculations. Today's computers form just one component of **information systems** capable of performing tasks that combine the important human function of communication with the ability to process mountains of data.

> **KEY POINT** Communication can take place on a global scale.

Understanding input, storage, processing, output and feedback is essential to all ICT examination courses.

Information systems can be described in terms of **inputs**, **storage**, **processing**, **outputs** and **feedback**. Data flows through an information system in these terms.

It is important to be clear about the difference between **data** and **information**. **Data** means the raw values entered into, stored and processed by information systems. **Information** is produced as output and feedback, with a context that gives it meaning.

In computing the word 'data' is used in the singular. Therefore in this context the sentence 'Data is entered into the system.' is correct, and 'Data are entered into the system.' is incorrect.

Data is usually a small piece of information. Data has to fit into a structure such as a sentence to give it meaning. The sentence 'Steve has a blue car' is an example. The words 'Steve', 'blue' and 'car' are data as are the letters that make up each word. None of these tell us anything on their own, but when put together into a sequence making up the words and sentences, they produce meaningful information.

Using ICT it is possible to structure data and information to make it simple to handle and easy to read. There are many ways in which information can be structured, such as text in a letter, names and addresses in database records and numbers in a table structure or spreadsheet.

The Information Superhighway

When people talk about the **Internet** (or the Net), they often also talk about two other things; the **World Wide Web** and the **Information Superhighway**.

You might think they are the same, but they are not.

The **Internet** is a network of networks, millions of computers exchanging information around the world. It supports **electronic mail** or **email**, **discussion groups**, files you can download to your computer and pages of information on the **World Wide Web**, often referred to as the Web.

The **Information Superhighway** is a creation of the politicians. It is an idea of how the world will be when everyone can connect, share information, and find out what is happening. It does not rely on the Internet, but the Net is the best way of making that information available now, even though sometimes the speed seems more like a horse and cart than a superhighway!

1.2 Inputs, processing and outputs

LEARNING SUMMARY

After completing this section you should be able to:

- *understand how a computer system works by describing its functions as inputs, processes and outputs*
- *understand how data is stored*

Functions of computer systems

OCR A   OCR B
EDEXCEL
AQA A   AQA B
NICCEA
WJEC

Make sure you can represent systems as simple block diagrams. This is an important aspect of answering examination questions.

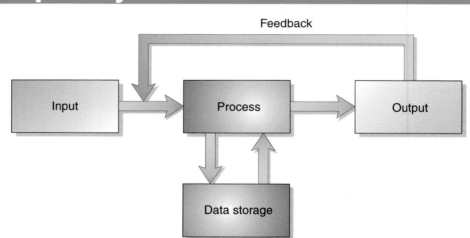

Inputs

Inputs are the raw data that is fed into an information system. The data is fed in via **input peripherals**, or **devices** – the machinery that makes it possible to feed in the values. There are a number of different ways of entering data.

Three examples are **keyboards**, **touch sensitive screens** and **scanners**. Input devices make use of human touch, sound, light, movement and magnetism.

Storage

Data is stored in an information system so that it can be utilised when required. It can be stored both **temporarily**, while a program is running, and **long-term**, so that it can be preserved while software and hardware is not in use.

Processing

This is the term used to describe the way information systems convert raw data into useful information. Processing includes the following functions: calculating; sorting; searching; storing; drawing. The name given to the processing unit in a computer is a **CPU** or central processing unit.

Outputs

Outputs are the visible or audible result of data processing – information that can be used. **Outputs** are made available by **output peripherals**, or devices – the machinery that makes them accessible to users. Examples of output devices are screens (both on computers and mobile phones), printers and speakers. Outputs can take the form of sounds, visual displays and movements.

Feedback

This term is used when output from a system is used to influence subsequent input.

PROGRESS CHECK

1. Describe the term 'input'.
2. State three input devices
3. State three output devices.
4. What is storage?
5. Is storage temporary or long term?

1. Raw data that is fed into an information system.   2. Keyboards, touch sensitive screens and scanners.   3. Screens, printers and speakers.   4. How an information system stores data so that it can be utilised when required.   5. It can be both temporary, while a program is running, and long-term, so that it can be preserved while software and hardware is not in use.

1.3 Data within information systems

LEARNING SUMMARY

After completing this section you should be able to:

● *understand the difference between analogue and digital signals*
● *know the difference between bits and bytes*

Analogue to digital conversion and digital to analogue

OCR A **OCR B**
WJEC

An electronic device is **digital** if data in it is represented as electrical 'on' and 'off' signals that correspond to binary digits and can be stored in computer memory.

Analogue

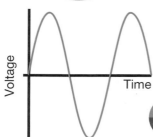

Voltage | Time

The data is therefore represented as a succession of 1s and 0s.

A device is **analogue** where data is represented as signals that vary within a predefined range. Traditional watch faces are analogue. The hands move continuously round a dial, within the predefined range of set seconds (0 to 60), minutes (0 to 60) and hours (12 or 24 in total). Time is represented by the position of the hands on the dial.

Many modern watches have a digital display, in which time is represented by the digits shown on a small display screen.

Digital signals have two **advantages**:

● they can be copied exactly, without even the slightest loss of quality
● they can be further processed by computer

KEY POINT All modern, general purpose computers are digital, but analogue computer circuits are used in industrial control equipment.

A digital computer is more accurate than an analogue computer because it only needs to sense the **difference** between clearly distinguishable states. For example, a slight fluctuation in electrical voltage would affect the result in an analogue computer but would not affect a digital computer because it could still easily distinguish the 1 state from the 0 state of any circuit element. For the same reason digital music reproduction (as on a compact disk) is more accurate than analogue reproduction (on a traditional vinyl record or cassette tape).

Digital

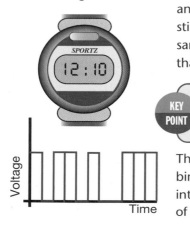

Voltage | Time

KEY POINT The term to 'digitise' means to convert data from an analogue form to a digital form so that it can be processed on a general purpose computer. See graphics digitiser and video digitiser (pages 22–23) and interfaces (page 28).

The system of using 1s and 0s to represent data on a digital computer is called binary format. Our standard counting system uses a base of 10. After 9, we move into double figures, and after 99, into three figures and so on. Binary is the base of 2. After 1, you move into double figures, after 11, into three figures and so on.

A **bit** is a binary digit – a 1 or 0 used to represent data. The term is also used for the smallest unit of storage, which just stores a 1 or a 0.

A **byte** is a small group of bits – normally eight bits – that is treated as a unit. It is usually the number of bits needed to store one character.

The main store of a computer, where data and instructions are held ready for use, is divided up into small, equally sized units called **locations**. The computer uses the unique address of a location to access it. Each storage location is full of 1s and 0s, which represent data in the form of:

> You do not need to memorise the exact numbers for bits and bytes but you should understand the differences, and how memory and data transfer times are affected by file size.

a number;
a character or string of characters;
a computer instruction;
part of a picture;
the address of a location in store.

> In most contexts, kilo stands for 1,000 and mega for 1,000,000. Because data is stored in binary format in computers, 'kilo' does not work, and the nearest power of 2 to these numbers is used instead.

K is short for kilo. 1 **Kb** is one **kilobyte** – 1024 bytes.

M is short for mega. 1 **Mb** is one **megabyte** – 1048576 bytes.

KEY POINT
● bit (binary digit – smallest data item)
● byte (8 bits)
● Kbyte (Kilo or 1 024 bytes – 2^{10})
● Mbyte (Mega or 1,048,576 or 2^{20})
● Gbyte (Giga or 1,073,741,824 or 2^{30})
● Terabyte ($\sim$1,099,000,000,000 or 2^{40})

PROGRESS CHECK

1. What is M short for?
2. What is a bit?
3. What is a byte?
4. What does 1KB mean?

1. Mega (1 048 576 bytes) – 1 Mb is one megabyte.   2. A binary digit – a 1 or 0 used to represent data. Also the smallest unit of storage, which just stores a 1 or a 0.   3. A small group of bits (usually 8) that are treated as a unit. Usually the number of bits needed to store one character.   4. One kilobyte (1 024 bytes).

Using information systems to aid communication

OCR A   OCR B
EDEXCEL
AQA A   AQA B
NICCEA
WJEC
Keys Skills

One of the main uses of ICT is to aid communication. Modern hardware and software programs allow the user to create attractive page layouts for databases, spreadsheets, documents and websites.

To develop communication skills, designers look at existing good practice and control the basic functions of the software to improve the presentation of text and graphics on their page or screen.

You will need to understand basic layouts for letters, memos, fax and websites.

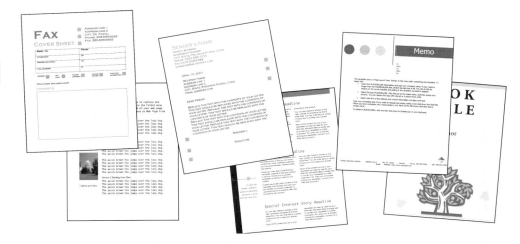

KEY POINT

To achieve a readable format designers divide the screen, page, or pages, into text and graphics. At this stage designers make decisions about the font types and size of main heading and sub-headings, column widths, and margins (side, top and bottom).

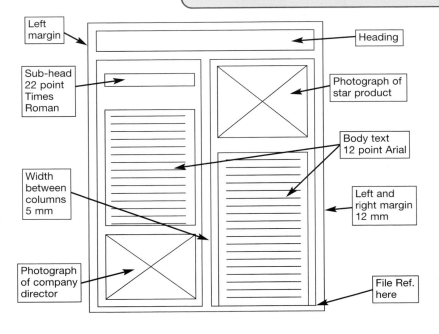

Left margin

Heading

Sub-head 22 point Times Roman

Photograph of star product

Body text 12 point Arial

Width between columns 5 mm

Left and right margin 12 mm

Photograph of company director

File Ref. here

All pages and screens can be split into what are called columns. Sometimes the text fits into one column like a book. Often, designers of printed and web-based pages divide the page into several columns. The illustration below shows a magazine and a number of web page layouts.

You should understand the terms and be able to identify columns, margins, headers and footers and describe page and screen layouts.

This two-column layout has an extra-wide space on the left. This can be used for hanging indents, which are helpful for scanning dense text in the right-hand column. The left-hand column can also include a frame for static information, such as a table of contents for the pages on the right.

This three-column layout is often use for annotations, images, even web frames. The middle column is centred and its size can be increased or decreased as needed.

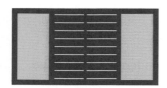

Four-column layouts are often used in newspapers and magazines. This layout is quite complex and can combine elements as described in the two previous grids.

Text can be placed on the columns in a number of ways.

Full justification arranges the text in a straight line on both the left- and right-hand margins.	Centre justified text is ragged on both sides but symmetrical in the centre of the page.	Text is justified to alter the balance of the page. This is right-justified text.	Left-justified text will be straight only on the left, leaving the text ragged on the right. This has the advantage of producing more regular word spacing.

Using text

OCR A   OCR B
EDEXCEL
AQA A   AQA B
NICCEA
WJEC
Keys Skills

It is generally better to restrict the number of typefaces and use variations on each one to distinguish different kinds of text, rather than using different typefaces.

We have seen that text can be laid out in different ways using margins and other graphic elements. The placing of graphics and text on a page helps to make the text readable and to communicate meaning. However, designers also need to explore changes brought about by altering certain groups of letters or words. A common procedure to create emphasis is to use letters of different sizes or weights.

In longer texts, this is often achieved by *using italics*. Headings are usually **bold**. The majority of fonts in common use have at least four variations in their families, e.g. normal, *italic*, **bold** and underlined. By combining these attributes others can be obtained such as ***bold italic***. Colour can also be added and type can be a variety of sizes measured in points.

26 Point lettering is larger than 14 point.

KEY POINT

An important factor in the production of a website or printed document is the selection of the correct typefaces. Choosing the right typeface clarifies the sense of the message. It also creates the right atmosphere or environment to help the reader understand the material more easily.

There are well over 32 unique type classifications and thousands of typefaces. Typefaces can be described in a number of ways, the two main categories being serif and sans serif.

Serif

Serif is an all-inclusive term for characters that have a line crossing the free end of a stroke.

ABCDEFGILM
NOPQRSTVX

Serif letter shapes based on ancient Roman lettering

Sans serif

Sans serif (*sans* meaning *without*) typeface have no line crossing the free end of a stroke.

ABCDEFGILM
NOPQRSTVX

Sample GCSE questions

1 Describe the computer term 'locations'.

The main store of a computer, where data and instructions are held ready for use, is divided up into small, equally sized units called locations. The computer uses the unique address of a location to access it. Each storage location is full of 1s and 0s, which represent data in binary format. **[4]**

2 Describe, using examples, how digital data and analogue data differ.

An electronic device is digital if data in it is represented as electrical `on´ and `off´ signals corresponding to binary digits and stored in computer memory. A device is analogue where data is represented as signals that vary within a predefined range. Traditional watch faces are analogue. **[4]**

Try to give examples if possible, e.g. an analogue watch face

3 Describe, using examples, why digital signals are more accurate than analogue when transmitted over a communication network.

A digital system only needs to sense the difference between clearly distinguishable states. For example, a slight fluctuation in electrical voltage would affect the result in an analogue computer but would not affect a digital computer because it could still easily distinguish the 1 state from the 0 state of any circuit element. For the same reason digital music reproduction (as on a compact disk) is more accurate than analogue reproduction (on a traditional vinyl record or cassette tape). **[4]**

Exam practice questions

1 Describe a system in terms of input, process, output and feedback.

....
....
....
....
.... **[10]**

2 Describe the difference between analogue and digital signals.

....
....
....
....
.... **[6]**

Hardware

The following topics are covered in this chapter:

- **2.1 Main components of a computer system**
- **2.2 Input peripherals or devices**
- **2.3 Output peripherals or devices**
- **2.4 Storage devices and media**

2.1 Main components of a computer system

LEARNING SUMMARY

After completing this section you should be able to:

- describe the main items of hardware that make up an information system
- understand that a computer forms one part of an information system
- describe the different forms that a computer can take, with typical uses
- describe the central processing unit of a computer, and its constituent parts

Computer systems

OCR A   OCR B
EDEXCEL
AQA A   AQA B
NICCEA
WJEC

A computer system is perhaps the most obvious example of an **information system**. The various devices that make up the system are called **hardware**. The computer itself may be a desktop, laptop, notebook, palmtop or PDA (personal digital assistant).

An easy way to think of the differences between data and information is to think that a computer can *process* data; it *produces* information.

Desktop (tower)

Laptop

Palmtop

The size of computers is being reduced all the time. For example, small, programmable devices that are called computers can be fitted inside cars to control the operation of the car, as well as carrying out other tasks such as direction finding. These have replaced the dedicated **micro-chips** that used to perform a similar, but more limited function. PDAs (personal digital assistants) are hand-held devices that can be used to help keep track of a busy working and social life.

PDAs offer functions such as:

- keeping track of appointments and regular commitments
- storing the names and addresses of contacts and friends
- downloading email from a personal computer so that it can be read offline on the PDA
- offering a full range of calculating facilities
- preparing, editing, sending and receiving faxes

Many modern day devices are controlled by micro-processors although it is not always obvious that they are. Examples include central heating systems, telephone systems and washing machines.

KEY POINT

As technology advances and micro-circuits get smaller these PDA systems are being built into mobile devices such as mobile telephones. Mobile telephones and televisions can therefore also form part of information systems. Where they can be programmed and allow interaction that can vary their function, they are essentially acting as computers.

A standard computer system used in an office or school situation consists of a number of components – the **computer** itself, and other **hardware devices** that are connected to it. These hardware devices are often referred to as **peripherals**. Details of peripherals that allow input of data and those that provide output of information are given later in this chapter.

The hardware typically supplied with a computer system includes the computer itself (containing one or more hard disk drives), a screen, a keyboard, a mouse and one or more additional disk and CD drives. The system can be represented as a simple block diagram.

The computer system described above is known as a **micro-computer** system. Mini-computer systems are larger and are used for many medium-sized commercial applications. For example, a traffic control system may use a mini-computer system.

See how the arrows have been used to indicate the nature of each device – whether it is an input or output device. You should always try to indicate your inputs and outputs using arrows.

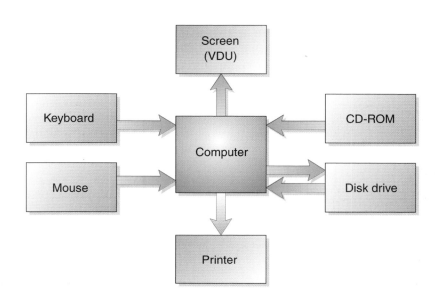

The largest computers are **main-frame** computers. These are used in situations where vast amounts of processing power and data storage ability are required. Banks, large insurance companies and utility companies such as suppliers of electricity and gas use main-frame computers.

These very powerful machines produce considerable amounts of heat, so that main-frame computer rooms have to be air conditioned. Some main-frames are water-cooled.

It is not just computers that contain microprocessors. Many everyday objects contain microprocessors which are pre-programmed to perform a dedicated task that is required by the device they control. There are chips in cars, washing machines, watches, laser printers and hand-held calculators. The name given to this type of ICT system is an embedded system.

Inside the computer

EDEXCEL
NICCEA
WJEC

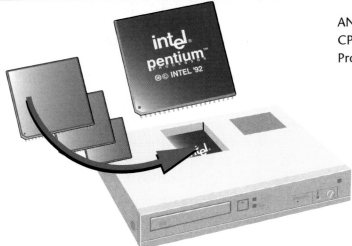

AN INTEL PROCESSOR
CPU (Central
Processing Unit)

> **You will not be expected to know how the components inside a computer work, but you will be expected to know about common components and their function.**

Any computer contains a **central processing unit**, where all instructions are carried out. The central processing unit can be described as the brain of the whole system.
It includes:

- the **control unit**, which controls the timing of operations and movement of data inside the computer, and between the computer and peripherals
- the **arithmetic and logic unit** (ALU), where calculations are performed and logical comparisons are made
- the **immediate access store** (IAS), which is the inbuilt memory of the computer system. It is also called primary, or main, store (see 2.4)

 PROGRESS CHECK

1. List the items of hardware that make up a typical computer system.
2. Describe what is meant by the term 'information system', explaining the role of a computer in the system.
3. What is the central processing unit of a computer? List its parts.

3. The part of a computer where all instructions are carried out. It is like the brain of the whole system and includes the control unit, the arithmetic and logic unit (ALU) and the immediate access store (IAS), which is also called primary, or main, store.
2. It is capable of performing, electronically, tasks that combine the important human function of communication with the ability to process mountains of data. A computer forms just one component of an information system.
1. The computer itself (containing one or more hard disk drives), a screen, a keyboard, a mouse and one or more additional disk and CD drives.

2.2 Input peripherals or devices

After completing this section you should be able to:

LEARNING SUMMARY

● explain what an input device is
● list the main types of input device, with their uses
● discuss the relative advantages and disadvantages of various input devices for particular tasks or users, or in terms of cost or other factors

Keyboards

OCR A OCR B
EDEXCEL
AQA A AQA B
NICCEA
WJEC

Keyboards come in a number of types. The standard keyboard and concept keyboard are the most common.

> Data can be input into an information system in a variety of ways. Most data is still in the form of text or numerals and is typed on keyboards.

Concept keyboard

OCR A OCR B
EDEXCEL
AQA A AQA B
NICCEA
WJEC

> Exam questions often ask about data input. Remember that there is more than one type of keyboard. A shop assistant and bar/restaurant staff do not need a full keyboard. Think about the type of data being entered and the environment the data entry takes place in.

A concept keyboard is a flat-bed or shaped set of contact switches covered by a **flexible membrane**. System and software designers can allocate one or more switches to respond in different ways. Often an **overlay** is placed over the keyboard with pictures or symbols.

Concept keyboards are popular for use with young children and anywhere that liquid may be spilt as they can be wiped clean. They are also used in restaurants, supermarkets, bars and cinemas. They are quick and easy to use as they utilise **Point and Touch** methods of data entry.

Special and concept keyboards are designed to enable people to enter computer data much more easily and quickly than with conventional keyboards.

Some concept and special keyboards are designed for young children or people with special needs for example:

- single handed keyboards for people with the use of only one hand
- single finger or Head/Mouth stick keyboards for people who do not have the use of a full hand
- expanded keyboards for physically disabled and visually impaired users

> **KEY POINT**
>
> **Point and touch methods are often used alongside keyboards, particularly for the following functions:**
> - **to make selections from menus or choose icons**
> - **to position the cursor on the screen**
> - **to produce graphics**
> - **to move images and create windows on the screen**

Standard keyboard

Keyboards

Standard

Ergonomic

Specialist keyboard

> **Different countries have different keyboard layouts to suit both specialist characters and the frequencies of letters used in typing in the specific language.**

The keys on a standard keyboard are:

- **Alphabet keys.** These represent all of the letters of the alphabet in lower case, unless the shift key (Caps Lock) is pressed to produce upper case. In countries such as France or Germany, where the language uses other letters more frequently, the arrangement of letters on the keyboard is different.

- **Digit keys.** These often appear twice: along the top main row of the main keyboard for keying mixed alphanumeric data, and on a number keypad to the right of the main keyboard for numeric data. Function of the number keypad can be switched on and off.

- **Other text characters** produce punctuation and mathematical symbols.

- **Cursor and other control characters.** These include:
  - arrow keys, the **TAB key** and keys such as **Page Up** and **Page Down**, for moving around documents
  - editing keys such as Insert and Delete
  - control keys such as Enter (Return) and Escape

> **A keyboard is still the most popular way of entering data.**

- **Keys that change the function of other keys.** These are the **shift key**, and those marked Caps Lock, Num Lock, Alt and Ctrl. The changes that these keys make may depend on the software being used.

- **Function keys.** These appear right at the top of the keyboard and are numbered F1 to F12. Their function is set by the program running and extra functions can usually be obtained by using the shift, Ctrl and Alt keys.

>
> **KEY POINT**
>
> **Advantages/Disadvantages of keyboards**
> - They are very reliable as a means of data input, both for alphabet characters and numerals, but not all users are able to type either quickly or accurately. Some people may be unable to use keyboards, e.g. if they suffer paralysis affecting their arms and hands. Specialised keyboards are available for use by disabled people. Concept keyboards are also available for particular uses.
> - Computers are normally supplied with keyboards so that it is not necessary to buy additional equipment.

Other point and touch input devices

OCR A **OCR B**
EDEXCEL
AQA A **AQA B**
NICCEA
WJEC

> You will be expected to know about a range of input point and touch devices, not just a mouse.

Mouse

A **mouse** is used on the desktop and translates its movements over a flat surface into digital information. In a traditional mouse the ball underneath the

Wheel mouse   Standard mouse

mouse rotates as the mouse is moved, and sensors pick up the movement. More modern mice use a beam of light rather than a ball to monitor movement.

The information gained from the movement is fed to the computer, causing the cursor to move on the screen. Mice usually have **one**, **two** or **three buttons** which are used to make selections on the screen.

A mouse is used, for example, to select **options** from a **menu** or from a **set of icons**, to position the cursor when editing text or using design software, to select an object in a drawing or a piece of text to be copied, moved or deleted.

A mouse is ideal for use with a desktop computer, typically in an office situation, but is not practical for use with a portable computer such as a **laptop**, **notebook** or **palmtop**.

One of the following two types of **point and touch** methods is normally used instead to achieve similar functions:

Touch sensitive pad

This is also known as a **track pad**. The user moves a stylus or finger across a pad and this moves the cursor on the screen.

> Both tracker balls and track pads take up less space than the mouse and normally form an integral part of a portable computer.

Tracker ball

A tracker ball is like an upside down mouse. The user rotates the ball but the 'mouse' part stays still.

Joystick

A joystick is similar to a tracker ball but does not form an integral part of the computer. When the lever is moved, the cursor moves in a similar direction on the screen.

The lever can be moved in any direction from its zero position. It can also be made to produce faster movements on the screen by pushing it further from the zero position.

Like the mouse, a joystick usually has buttons with which actions can be carried out once the cursor is in the right place. Some joysticks can be rotated to give even more control on the screen.

Joysticks are mainly used for computer games as they allow the fast interaction that is needed in this context. They are also used, for example, with ultrasound scanners in hospitals, and for producing other types of graphics.

Joystick

Light pen

A screen **cursor** can be moved by touching the screen with a **light pen**. Special software is required to make light pens work, and they are mainly used for design work.

Light pen

Touch sensitive screen

A screen through which data can by entered into a computer by touching it with a finger. Items are selected as they would be with a mouse or light pen. Touch sensitive screens usually work by means of criss-crossing beams of infra-red light just in front of the glass. When the user touches the glass two sets of rays are blocked giving an x and y axis. Most interactive whiteboards work in a similar way to this.

Touch sensitive screens are ideal in museums, shops and Internet booths. They are easy to use and ideal for information kiosks.

KEY POINT

Advantages/Disadvantages of touch screens compared with other point and touch methods

- The advantage of a touch screen is that no extra peripherals are needed except the monitor, although this has to be adapted to respond to touch. The touch method is very useful in situations where a keyboard or mouse could become dirty or wet, and where users are standing and moving about.
- A disadvantage is that the touch screen is not suitable for inputting large quantities of data.

Inputting mainly graphics/images

OCR A | OCR B
EDEXCEL
AQA A | AQA B
NICCEA
WJEC

Most users consider a graphics digitiser to be the best current method of allowing freehand drawings to be entered into the computer but a mouse can also be used.

Graphics digitiser

A **graphics digitiser**, or **tablet**, is a board with a surface that resembles electronic tracing paper. Like paper, it is available in a range of sizes from A4 to a very large A10 size that would cover most of an office desk. A **cursor**, or puck, is used on a graphics digitiser to trace over a technical drawing. As the cursor is moved, pressure on the surface is detected and data about position (x and y coordinates) is sent to the computer using computer aided design software such as AutoCAD.

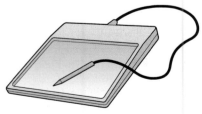
Graphic digitiser

Video digitiser

A video digitiser is used to convert a **video picture** into a **computer image**. A video camera is used to produce a picture. The **digitiser**, a combination of **hardware** and **software**, converts the **analogue video signal** into a digital signal in the computer's memory. Each frame from a video is converted so that it can be played back or printed in any required sequence. The stored image can be used in the same way as any other graphic. When stored it uses a large amount of disk space.

Think carefully before you label or select an input device. What is required in terms of resolution, speed etc? How skilled will the operator be?

- Video digitising is used to capture a frame from a video sequence so that it can be printed in a document or magazine, and in making television adverts and pop videos.

Scanner

Scanners are able to detect pictures as a series of dots on a page.

A scanner is a device used to examine methodically, or scan, pictures, text, or other information and send them to the computer as accessible data. The data can then be manipulated in some way before being printed.

Scanners

Hand held

Flat-bed desktop

An OCR system is a scanner with appropriate software.

An optical mark reader is a scanner with appropriate software.

There are two main types of scanner:

- **hand-held devices** that are moved across the source material being scanned
- more expensive **flat-bed scanners**

The source material, for example a picture, is laid on the scanner bed and the device remains stationary while the picture is scanned. This type of scanning is very accurate, giving a high range of resolution as every dot of a picture is stored. As with video images, however, scanned images take up a lot of disk space.

In choosing between a hand-held and desktop scanner or a digital camera think about the desired input. A camera is best for three-dimensional objects, a scanner is best for two-dimensional objects.

> **KEY POINT**
>
> Scanners are often supplied with OCR (optical character recognition) software. This enables them to scan text, recognising each of the characters separately so that they can be edited using word processing software.

Digital camera

A **digital camera** is used to take photographs in the same way as a traditional camera, except that it does not use **light sensitive**

Digital camera

Memory card

The amount of memory taken up by a stored picture depends on its resolution. This is determined by the number of dots that make up the picture. The more dots, the sharper the image, and the more memory that will be used up.

film. The digital camera has a memory in which images are stored and extra **memory cards** can be bought to increase the camera's storage capacity. The more memory the camera has, the more pictures can be taken before it is necessary to download onto a computer.

On most digital cameras, the user can see the picture that has just been taken on a small screen at the back and, if the image is not suitable, can delete it straight away.

Pictures are downloaded onto a computer by means of a cable between the camera and computer, or by placing the camera near to the computer and using **infra-red** technology to make the two devices communicate, or by removing the memory disk from the camera, plugging it into the computer and using a reader to interpret the data.

Some cameras are left permanently linked to computers, positioned so that users can collect pictures of themselves. The image data can then be transmitted with voice data or text messages to allow video conferencing to take place.

> Specialised software is required to edit, store and display pictures on the computer.

KEY POINT

Advantages of digital cameras
- no film is needed, and there are no expensive developing costs
- unwanted images can be deleted immediately
- photographic images can be put into a document without the need for a scanner
- since pictures are in digital form, they can be transmitted via Internet
- images can be edited without the need for professional darkroom work. Specialised software such as PhotoShop allows users to remove unwanted details in photographs, add extra features and adjust colour and contrast.

Automated input devices

OCR A   OCR B
EDEXCEL
AQA A   AQA B
NICCEA
WJEC

> Each code has separate left and right halves which can be read in either direction.

Bar codes and readers

0376-8929(200003)

Bar codes are used in most supermarkets and libraries, in luggage handling systems at airports and for warehouse stock control. Each item of stock is marked with a unique code composed of dark and light bars of different widths.

The code represents a number, which is the data to be fed into the computer system. The **bar code reader** detects the amount of light reflected by the dark and light lines in the bar code, and many readers are now so sensitive that they can read a code from a distance of five metres or more.

In supermarkets and warehouse situations, the reading of bar codes allows computer systems to keep stock levels up to date so that goods can be re-ordered as soon as they are required.

- Useful data about demand can also be obtained, for example which item in a particular range is selling best. In libraries, each book is marked with a code, and borrower tickets also have a code which allows the computer system to match borrowers with books and return dates. A similar system is operated with items of luggage and their owners at airports.

KEY POINT

It is possible for a barcode reader to misread a bar code, for example if there is a dirty mark on the code. For this reason a check digit calculated from all the other figures in the code is attached to the rest of the code when it is printed. The scanning system normally beeps when data has been accepted and remains quiet when it has not, in which case the code can be typed in using a keyboard.

BLOCK VII

1	—A—B—C—D—E—F—G—
2	—A—B—C—D—E—F—G—
3	—A—B—C—D—E—F—G—
4	—A—B—C—D—E—F—G—

Optical mark readers and optical mark recognition (OMR)

Optical mark readers are able to sense marks made on pre-printed forms in certain places. Typical uses include multiple choice answer sheet marking, capturing data from questionnaires, enrolment forms and lottery tickets, and the checking of football pools coupons.

An answer form for a multiple choice examination provides a good example of an OMR form. The person taking the examination makes a dark pencil mark in the space provided for the answer he or she thinks is right. The printing already on the form is in very pale ink called fade-out ink. This is not detected by the mark reader, which will pick up only the dark pencil marks. It does this by detecting the amount of light reflected from different parts of the form. The dark marks reflect less light. The mark reader transmits data about each space to the computer, and the software works out whether answers are right or wrong, and adds up the total mark.

> Be careful not to confuse optical mark readers (OMR) and optical character recognition (OCR).

KEY POINT

Advantages/Disadvantages of optical mark readers

- The principal disadvantages of optical mark readers are that the forms must be completed clearly and in accordance with precise instructions, otherwise they will not be read correctly. Secondly, any damage – creasing, folding or dirt – may prevent forms from being read correctly.
- The use of OMR in many contexts has the advantage that details do not have to be typed in. Typing takes time and can introduce errors. OMR also reduces the cost of inputting large volumes of data because people do not need to type the details. Finally, the method is useful when results of tests are needed quickly, for example with an aptitude test for a job.

Optical character readers and optical character recognition (OCR)

An **optical character reader** also works by detecting the amount of light reflected from a sheet of paper. A scanner is used with specialised software that transmits data about the pattern of light and dark areas on the paper to the computer, converting the scanned image into standard **ASCII code**. The pattern of data is compared with stored patterns for different characters. The best match is selected and the code representing the character is stored. As each individual letter has been recognised on its own, it can be edited later using word processing software.

> OCR software can be used to scan financial documents such as company accounts direct into spreadsheets, as well as to scan text direct into word processors.

Disadvantages of optical character readers

- Optical character readers do not work well with hand written text, as they have to be able to recognise the difference between, for example, an S and a 5, or a B and an 8. It is best if the text is typed, and in a standard font, as different fonts, type sizes and upper and lower case letters may all pose problems.

KEY POINT

Magnetic ink character readers and magnetic character recognition (MICR)

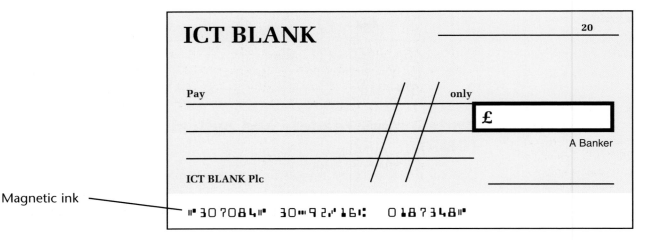

ICT BLANK

20

Pay _____ only

£

A Banker

ICT BLANK Plc

Magnetic ink —

⑊307084⑊ 30⑊92⑊16⑊ 0187348⑊

Magnetic ink character recognition is used in banking. Magnetic ink characters are the numbers found along the bottom of cheques. They indicate the account number, branch code and cheque number. The characters are printed using an ink that contains iron and may be magnetised. The magnetic pattern of the numbers is read by a magnetic ink character reader. A standard character set is used to print the numbers, so that comparisons are simple and reading is fast.

> **KEY POINT**
>
> **Advantages/Disadvantages of MICR**
> - MICR is accurate and secure, but it uses expensive equipment and is suitable only for very large scale applications. This factor is an advantage in banking as the cost would make it unlikely that other people would be able to build the equipment and print their own cheques.
> - When a person pays a cheque into a bank, the bank must add the amount to the cheque in magnetic ink before the cheque can be passed through the banking system.

Magnetic strips and readers

> The amount of data that can be stored on a strip is limited.

Strips of magnetisable material can be built into plastic cards such as credit cards and bank guarantee cards. These strips can be magnetised to store data, typically the account number and expiry date of the card.

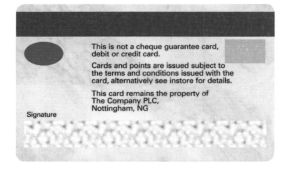

This is not a cheque guarantee card, debit or credit card.

Cards and points are issued subject to the terms and conditions issued with the card, alternatively see instore for details.

This card remains the property of The Company PLC, Nottingham, NG

Signature

Magnetic strip readers are found at the side of computerised tills and are used to read information contained in the magnetic strips on cards. The readers detect the pattern of magnetisation and convert it to numeric data and reading is accurate and fast.

> **KEY POINT**
>
> **Advantages/Disadvantages of magnetic strips**
> - The cards work well but are easily damaged. Exposure to a strong magnet, such as those used, for example, to remove security tags in shops, can alter the magnetic pattern representing the vital data on a card. The reader will then be unable to pick up the data and the numbers have to be typed in by hand.

EPOS and EFTPOS terminals – input *and* output devices

OCR A   OCR B
EDEXCEL
AQA A   AQA B
WJEC

EPOS terminals

EPOS (**electronic point of sale**) terminals are the cash registers commonly found in retail outlets that also act as terminals to the main computer of the retail outlet. Data about goods being sold is fed into the terminals, normally via barcode readers, touch screens and keyboards and, as well as providing customers with itemised bills, these systems also generate useful management information.

EFTPOS terminals

Always use examples when answering questions on EPOS and EFTPOS. Talk about the supermarket or shop to show the examiner that you really understand the application and use of the technology.

EFTPOS terminals are similar to **EPOS terminals** but with some additional features. They are able to transfer funds from a customer's bank account direct to a retail outlet's account after reading the customer's debit card. This provides a much faster method of payment than cheques and credit cards.

KEY POINT

Disadvantages
- There is a risk, however, of debit cards being stolen or forged and some people believe that, like credit cards, they encourage people to spend more.

Sensors and remote sensors

OCR A   OCR B
EDEXCEL
AQA A   AQA B
NICCEA
WJEC

Some exam questions focus upon how to capture usable data from remote sensors. Remember the difference between analogue and digital signals. It will form a key part of this type of question.

Sensors are input devices that are used to detect external changes in an environment. They may register levels of light, temperature, sound, or proximity, position, pH balance or humidity.

The data received is converted to **digital values** and transmitted to the computer system. The data can be processed immediately, to influence outputs from the system, or it can be stored for later analysis.

Further common examples of the use of sensors are at traffic lights and pedestrian crossings, to detect the presence of vehicles or people, and in freezer and chiller cabinets in supermarkets, to monitor temperature.

Sensors are often located at some distance from the computer system to which they are sending data. In this case they are known as **remote sensors**. Their electronic signals are sent through telephone wires or via radio transmitters to a computer that could be located in another part of the world.

KEY POINT

Remote sensors are used in weather stations, where temperature, pressure and wind speed can be detected at many isolated locations, and the data then sent to a central computer. In a similar way, water authorities may use remote sensors to monitor the level of water or pollution in rivers and reservoirs.

Input devices that register sound

> The user must train the software to recognise his or her voice and speech pattern, but, until the software becomes more sophisticated, there is a possibility that some words will be interpreted incorrectly.

> Apart from speech, a microphone can detect music or any other kind of sound that can be transmitted to the computer's memory.

Microphone and speech recognition software

A microphone is used as the input device for a **speech recognition system**. The sound is detected by the microphone and a varying electrical signal is transmitted to the computer. Specialised hardware is used to convert this **analogue** data into **digital data** that can be stored. Speech recognition software will then convert the words into text in a word processing program.

Speech recognition software improved considerably when the developers started to produce software that would listen to whole sentences and phrases rather than individual words.

A microphone may also be used as an **input device** to a voice mail system. **Voice mail** uses the Internet to send, store and receive voice messages. The Internet service provider (the company providing connection to the Internet) stores the voice message on its server and when the user logs on, the system informs them that they have a voice mail message. The user can then play back the message using a **loudspeaker** as an **output device**.

KEY POINT

> **Advantages/Disadvantages of speech recognition software**
> ● The software has to be trained to recognise the speech pattern of each individual user. It works best with a special microphone positioned just centimetres below the mouth, as this avoids picking up surrounding noise or breathing sounds. The software must also be trained to recognise specialist or technical words that may not feature in a normal vocabulary. Users of speech recognition software may also have to be trained as many people find it difficult to speak in a 'writing' style.

MIDI

> An organised series of MIDI commands is called a sequence.

MIDI stands for **musical instrument digital interface**. A MIDI uses hardware and software to connect an electronic musical instrument such as a keyboard, **synthesiser** or drum machine to a computer. The frequency, pitch and other musical data received is converted to digital data which can be read by the computer. Music played on the instrument can therefore be stored on the computer, which can, in turn, send signals back to the instrument.

MIDI systems are also used to control specialised devices such as theatrical lighting.

PROGRESS CHECK

1. What is an input device?
2. What forms can the data take?
3. What are the main types of input device?
4. What are the advantages of touch screens over other point and touch methods of inputting data?
5. Name one disadvantage of touch screens over other point and touch methods of inputting data.

1. A machine that provides a means of feeding data into a computer. The input device receives the data from a human operator or from a sensor and passes it to the central processing unit.
2. Numbers or characters (alphabet letters), sound or pictures.
3. The main types are keyboards, point and touch methods such as mice, touch sensitive pads and touch sensitive screens, graphics digitisers, video digitisers, scanners, digital cameras, automated input devices such as bar code readers and optical mark or character readers, and devices that register sound.
4. No extra peripherals are needed except the monitor, although this must be adapted to respond to touch. The touch method is very useful where a keyboard or mouse could become dirty or wet, and where users are standing and moving about. Touch screens are easy to use and operators do not need good keyboard skills to use them.
5. Touch screens are not suitable for inputting large quantities of data.

2.3 *Output peripherals or devices*

LEARNING SUMMARY

After completing this section you should be able to:

- *explain what an output device is*
- *list the main types of output device, with their uses: monitors / screens, printers and plotters, audible output devices, control devices*
- *discuss the relative advantages and disadvantages of various output devices for particular tasks or users, or in terms of cost or other factors*
- *understand what permanent copy is, and say whether an output device produces permanent copy*

As with input devices think carefully before answering exam questions about output devices. What data output is required and who will read it? What environment is the system functioning in?

Output devices provide information in an accessible form after **data processing**.

Monitor/screen

OCR A OCR B
EDEXCEL
AQA A AQA B
NICCEA
WJEC

Every desktop computer, most portables, electronic calculators and mobile phones have a **display screen** of some kind. On a desktop computer, the screen is often known as the **monitor**, or as a **VDU** (**visual display unit**). Screens are available in various sizes.

Standard **VDUs** on desktop computers work in the same way as the screen on a standard television set, but this technology is too bulky for portables or the other hand-held devices. These use liquid crystal displays, made from flat plates with liquid between them.

Although liquid crystal displays take up much less space, the disadvantage is that these screens can be viewed only from a limited angle. As the technology improves, flat screen panels are becoming available for desktop computers too.

A screen display is either **monochrome**, or **colour**.

Monochrome does not necessarily mean black and white. They may have orange or green text on a black background, the significant difference being that they do not provide the range of colour of a colour screen.

Screens are measured on the diagonal. In other words, a 17 inch screen will measure 17 inches from the top left corner to the bottom right.

Monochrome screens are suitable where they are used only to provide **text displays**. Colour is considered to be more restful to the eye and is necessary to show detail of graphics, or to highlight **error messages**, menu options, etc in **word processing**. However, the use of colour takes up more storage space and requires more processing time.

KEY POINT The resolution of a monitor, or screen, is very important. This relates to the clarity of the image on the screen and is defined by the number of separate units of light (known as pixels) across and down the screen that can be displayed. A pixel is square in shape and represents the smallest area of the screen which the computer can change. For some applications, such as computer aided design (CAD) and desktop publishing, a high resolution screen is required, or images will not be sufficiently clear.

The higher the resolution of a display, the more pixels are used. This takes up more storage space in the computer. High resolution images also take longer to process and a fast processor is required to animate a high resolution picture smoothly.

A flat screen monitor

It is possible to use a method called **interlacing** to produce a screen image which seems to have a higher resolution than the screen can display. However, this results in more screen flicker than a display that has not been interlaced.

The **flat screens** that are now becoming available offer better quality with less flicker, and they take up less space.

KEY POINT **Advantages/Disadvantages of screens as output devices**
- The principal disadvantage is that they do not provide permanent copy. They are also unsuitable for any users with visual problems.
- Advantages are that they provide high speed change of display, which can include text, graphics and colours. They make no noise and do not waste paper.

Printers (laser, ink-jet, dot matrix)

OCR A OCR B
EDEXCEL
AQA A AQA B
NICCEA
WJEC

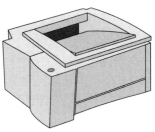

Laser

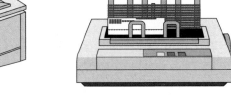

Dot matrix

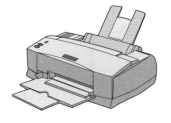

Ink-jet

Printers provide output in the form of permanent copy, normally on paper. Many can also print on to acetate sheets that are used on overhead projectors.

Exam questions often ask you to say what the best printer for a given situation is. You do not need to understand how each printer works but you should know the advantages and disadvantages of each type of printer.

Printers are chosen because of their purchase and running cost alongside their printing speed and resolution. Printing speeds are usually expressed as the number of pages per minute. Resolution is often expressed in terms of the number of dots per inch (dpi). The larger the number of dots the higher the resolution.

All printers use consumables that need replacing. These can take the form of the paper, card or acetate they print on and the inks, ribbons or toner they use to form the printed image. Some printers, such as ink-jet printers need special coated papers to achieve the best results. These are more expensive and add to the running costs.

> **KEY POINT**
> There are three established types of printer, although new types are being developed. The three standard types are: dot matrix, ink-jet and laser.

Impact printers

OCR A OCR B
EDEXCEL
AQA A AQA B
WJEC

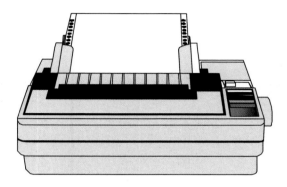

Dot matrix printers

Dot matrix printers were the first type to be developed for use in computer systems. They are **impact printers**, producing output by hammering pins or character patterns against a ribbon and the paper. This means that they are able to print multi-part stationery such as invoice sets used by many companies, where a number of copies are required.

Dot matrix printers use a ribbon impregnated with ink to transfer the image or text on to paper. This ribbon needs changing when the ink is used up or it dries out.

> **KEY POINT**
> **Disadvantage of dot matrix printers**
> ● They are noisy and produce a low quality of printout and, for these reasons, have largely been replaced by either ink-jets or lasers.

Golf ball printers

Golf ball printers use a rotating sphere of letters to produce high quality print. They are suitable only for printing **alpha-numeric characters** and cannot produce graphics.

> **KEY POINT**
> **Advantage of golf ball printers**
> ● The quality of output through an impact printer that is capable of printing multi-part stationery.

Non-impact printers

OCR A OCR B
EDEXCEL
AQA A AQA B
WJEC

Ink-jet and lasers are non-impact printers.

> **KEY POINT**
> **Advantages of non-impact printers**
> ● They are quiet when working and produce high quality output. They can all produce graphics and most types are capable of producing colour.

Laser printers

A laser printer uses a laser beam to build up an electrical image of a page on a light sensitive drum in the same way as a **photocopier**. The image is built up from dots.

Colour laser printers use three-colour toner cartridges – cyan, magenta and yellow – plus black.

Early laser printers used 300 dots to the inch, but the latest printers use at least 600 dots to the inch (2.5 cm) so that the individual dots cannot be seen. Once the image has been formed on the drum, a plastic powder called **toner** is held against the paper in the same pattern. The paper and toner are heated to fix the powder to the paper.

Laser printer toner is supplied in cartridges that need replacing when the toner runs out. Colour laser printers have four toner cartridges. Laser printers are expensive to buy compared with other types of printer but they are fast and cheap to run as they print on standard paper. Toner cartridges are expensive compared with other printer consumables but they cost less per page than other printers as the toner cartridges print a large number of copies before they need changing.

KEY POINT

Advantages/disadvantages of laser printers:
- Laser printers are fast and produce high quality output. They are expensive, however, particularly colour laser printers. Toner cartridges have to be replaced as soon as they run out and may also be expensive. Some suppliers operate schemes for recycling used toner cartridges.

Ink-jet printers

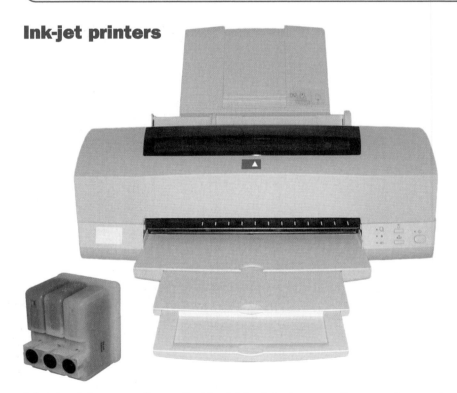

Ink-jet printers are often called **bubble-jets** because they produce output by spraying tiny drops of ink on to the paper. The print head of an ink-jet printer consists of nozzles through which ink flows and is heated, to form bubbles. Each bubble expands and breaks, releasing a tiny ink droplet. The dots formed are smaller and more numerous (usually between 300 and 800 dots to the inch) than those produced by a dot matrix printer.

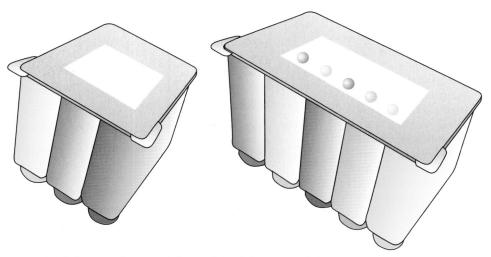

A standard three colour and five colour ink-jet cartridge

- Ink-jet printers work well on ordinary paper, giving high quality output.
- Standard ink-jet printers have three-colour cartridges, plus a black cartridge. Ink-jet printers designed to produce photographic quality output have five-colour cartridges, plus black.

Ink-jet cartridges are quite cheap to buy but they do not last very long. As special paper is required for a high quality colour printout, ink-jet printers are quite expensive to use in comparison with other types of printer. This is balanced out by the fact that the printers themselves are quite cheap to buy.

> **KEY POINT**
>
> **Advantages/disadvantages of ink-jet printers:**
> - Colour ink-jet printers can produce images that are almost as good as photographs if they are printed on high quality paper.
> - The ink-jet system does not work well, however, on any paper that is absorbent as the wet ink droplets tend to spread before they can dry.
> - Ink-jets are slower than laser printers but less expensive to buy.
> - Running costs are usually higher than for lasers as high quality printing paper is costly and ink cartridges, especially colour cartridges, can be expensive and do not last long under certain conditions of use.
> - Ink-jet printers normally take up less space than laser printers and are almost silent in operation.

Plotters

OCR A   OCR B
EDEXCEL
AQA A   AQA B
NICCEA
WJEC

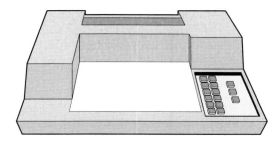

Flat-bed plotter

A **plotter** is a device for producing high quality graphical output on paper. It can produce plans, maps, line diagrams and three dimensional drawings. Plotters come in sizes that match the standard sizes of paper, and can be very large.

There are two main types of plotter, **pen plotters** and **penless plotters**. Penless plotters use various different technologies. High quality work for publication is produced by electrostatic plotters.

On a flat-bed plotter, the paper is held stationary on a flat surface. On a large flat-bed plotter, the paper may be held in place by suction from underneath. On a drum plotter, the paper, usually in a roll, is held on a drum that can be rotated backwards and forwards.

- Pen plotters use pens to produce images and different pens may be used, containing different coloured inks.
- The pens can reach any point on the piece of paper.
- The lines drawn are continuous, not made of dots, and the drawing produced is very accurate.
- Pen plotters may be classified as either flat-bed plotters, or drum plotters.
- The pens used in plotters need to be replaced when they run out of ink.

KEY POINT

Advantages/disadvantages of plotters:
- **Output is slow from a plotter, but speed is less important than accuracy for the type of graphics it produces. Technical drawings for a car, for example, must be accurate.**

Speakers and voice synthesis

OCR A   OCR B
EDEXCEL
AQA A   AQA B
NICCEA
WJEC

Voices can be synthesised by storing word patterns as bit strings. When the computer has to 'speak', the appropriate codes are sent to a voice response unit that produces the sounds.

The **output devices** described so far produce visual output. Speakers produce audible output and work in the same way as speakers used with music systems. Computer systems that are designed to run **multimedia** software are often supplied with speakers as an integral part. On other systems, the speakers are connected by cables to special hardware fitted inside the computer casing.

Apart from playing back music and other sound, speakers can produce voice output. This is invaluable for visually handicapped users. Voice output is generally more successful than **voice recognition** at the input stage.

Voice synthesis can be used to produce output from a computer via a telephone without the need for a modem or a terminal. Codes can be sent by pressing combinations of the buttons on the telephone, prompting the computer to reply with **synthesised** speech.

A number of small, hand-held electronic devices are available that use small speakers to produce synthesised speech. They include language translators and small learning aids, for example to help children with arithmetic.

KEY POINT

Advantages/disadvantages of audible output devices:
- **Audible output is ideal for those who are visually handicapped. It requires no reading ability and can be accessed by telephone.**
- **Disadvantages are that it is not suitable for use in noisy environments, nor in very quiet environments where other people are working. No permanent copy is produced and there can be some difficulty understanding messages. If a message is not understood the first time, the computer can only repeat it in exactly the same way, so that it may not be understood the second time either.**

Control devices

OCR A   OCR B
EDEXCEL
AQA A   AQA B
NICCEA
WJEC

Some output devices provide permanent copy while others do not.

Output can be used to **control devices** such as lights, buzzers, robots and actuators (hardware devices such as motors). The output operates parts such as switches and hydraulic systems in these devices. For example, an actuator motor might be used to open a window in a greenhouse when a temperature sensor has registered that it has got too hot.

**PROGRESS
CHECK**

1. What is an output device?
2. List the main types of output device.
3. What are the advantages of screens as output devices?
4. What is the principal disadvantage of screens as output devices?
5. What are the advantages of audible output devices?
6. Explain what permanent copy is.

1. A machine, linked to a computer, that shows, prints or presents the results of a computer's work.
2. Monitors/screens, printers and plotters, audible output devices, control devices.
3. They provide high speed change of display, which can include text, graphics and colours. They make no noise and do not waste paper.
4. They do not provide permanent copy. They are also unsuitable for any users with visual problems.
5. They are ideal for those who are visually handicapped. They require no reading ability and can be accessed by telephone.
6. Computer output that has been produced in a form in which it can be kept and stored. The commonest examples are printed written documents, printed drawings or other graphical output.

2.4 Storage devices and media

**LEARNING
SUMMARY**

After completing this section you should be able to:

- *explain what a storage device is, including the difference between main store memory and backing stores*
- *describe the functions of memory in a computer system*
- *understand the difference between volatile and non-volatile memory*
- *describe the features of ROM and RAM, the two types of main store memory*
- *describe the main types of backing stores, with their uses: hard disks, floppy disks, CD-ROMs, CD-Rs, CD-RWs, magnetic tape, DVDs*

Main store memory

OCR A   OCR B
EDEXCEL
AQA A   AQA B
NICCEA
WJEC

ROM, RAM

A standard computer forms the central part of an information system and its **central processing** unit has two types of memory, or main store. These are **read-only memory (ROM)** and **random access memory (RAM)**.

Memory, or main store, is the term used for the group of chips inside the processing unit where data is held temporarily while processing takes place. This memory is instantly accessible, unlike backing storage which is held outside the central processing unit and has to be accessed on disk or tape.

> **KEY POINT**
>
> Memory is used for the following functions:
> - to hold programs – these may be the operating system (programs which control the hardware) or applications programs (programs that fulfil a particular user-related task such as database creation)
> - to hold data that has been input
> - to provide a working area to store data that is currently being processed
> - to hold output data before it is sent to an output device

Exam questions will often ask why a particular type of storage is not suitable to a given circumstance, e.g. why a CD-ROM is not suitable for a dentist database.

Remember the acronyms RAM and ROM and what the letters stand for.

All the internal components of a computer are usually placed on what is called the motherboard.

The memory required to run programs has increased enormously as more icons, colour and graphics are used.

Exam questions often relate to the differences between volatile and non-volatile memory.

Characteristics of the main store are that data can be written and read at very high speeds. It can be transferred without any mechanical movement. The main store is divided into **locations** and usually contains two different types of memory:

> Most of the memory in a computer system is usually RAM.

Read Only Memory (ROM)

Data stored on ROM is held even when the power is switched off and is therefore considered to be non-volatile memory.

This is held on a chip inside the **processor** and is used to hold data that cannot be changed by the user. Programs related to the operating system are stored on ROM chips when a computer is manufactured. This data will usually be the software that tells the computer how to load the **operating system** (called the **boot program**) when it is switched on or re-booted.

Random Access Memory (RAM)

In contrast to ROM, **RAM** is **volatile** memory. It is held on a chip, but only temporarily. The data held disappears if the power is switched off. RAM is used to hold both data and programs during **processing**. It also holds the contents of the screen during use.

Printers normally contain some **RAM**, to store the next set of data to be printed, and some ROM to store programs to control the printing process, and to hold the shapes of different fonts.

Backing stores

OCR A   OCR B
EDEXCEL
AQA A   AQA B
NICCEA
WJEC

Access to backing stores is slightly slower than to main store, but the data held is non-volatile. It is stored until it is deleted.

Backing stores hold data outside the **central processing** unit in some kind of storage medium. The commonest types of storage media are hard disks, floppy disks and CD-ROMs. When the user wishes to have access to the data, the storage medium must be inserted into a drive in the processing unit, where read/write heads transfer the data to main store RAM.

Storage media are compared using the following criteria:

- volatility (will data be lost when power is removed?)
- storage capacity (how much data can they hold?)
- speed of access and retrieval (how fast can they be read or written to?)
- read capability (how easy is it to read the data on them and what special hardware and software is needed?)
- write capability (how easy is it to write the data on them and what special hardware and software is needed?)
- cost

Hard disks and floppy disks are magnetic storage media. Data is held as magnetised spots on the disk surface. The spot is magnetised in one direction to represent a binary 1 and in a different direction to represent a binary 0. Each bit (see 1.3) is stored separately and the data is arranged in circular tracks, divided into sectors, on the disk surface.

Hard disks

A hard disk is the main storage device in most computer systems.

Hard disks are made of metal coated with a magnetisable material. They can hold a large amount of data (more than floppy disks) and are usually fixed inside the hard disk drive of the **computer**. This will usually hold several disks on a single spindle. As each disk surface is able to store data, each surface can have its own **read/write head**. These can operate

Hard drive

simultaneously, which means that data can be transferred and utilised more quickly than by using a single larger disk. This **access time** is very important because modern software often needs to move data to and from a hard disk. It does not hold everything in **memory** all the time.

A read/write head can both read data from the storage medium and write data to the storage medium. A read-only head can read data but not modify or save data to the storage medium.

Even if the computer has a fast processor, if access time to the hard disks is slow, the software will not run properly.

Hard disks are used to:
- store the operating system, applications software and user's files for a PC
- store the operating system, software and files for a local area network (LAN)
- store work awaiting printing

Exam questions often ask you to state what type of media various types of data should be stored on.

The **read/write** heads move across the disk extremely close to the surface. A speck of dust can easily cause damage and for this reason it is normal to seal the hard disks inside the disk drive. This also keeps moisture away from the disk's surface.

Floppy disks

Floppy disks can vary in size but the commonest is 3.5 inches.

Floppy disks are made of plastic coated with a **magnetisable** material. They are sealed into a protective case with openings to allow data to be **written** and **read**. The case can be made of card, but the most commonly used disks have rigid plastic cases.

Before a floppy disk can be used to store data, it must be formatted. This creates a magnetic map of the disk surface so that data can be read from the disk or written on to it quickly.

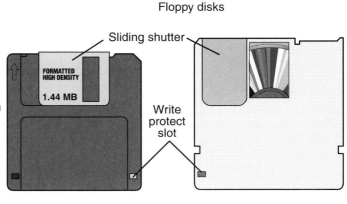

Floppy disks

Sliding shutter

FORMATTED HIGH DENSITY

1.44 MB

Write protect slot

Standard floppy   Super 'optical' disk

Floppy disks are sometimes used to supply **applications packages** to users, but because their **capacity** is relatively small, each package normally takes up several disks. For this reason most **programs** are now supplied on CD-ROM. It is rare for programs to be run from floppy disks. They are normally installed on to the **hard drive** first. This makes access much simpler and faster.

> **KEY POINT**
>
> Floppy disks are useful for holding data files, as long as they are not too big, and they are used to hold back-up copies of the data and programs on the hard disks. A new generation of floppy disks, sometimes called super disks, can hold a larger amount of data. The most common super disks hold 120 Mb of data. All floppy disks are light and portable, easy to exchange and transport.

You will need to understand different ways of backing up data. Often questions on security issues expect you to refer to data backup. Try to include the name of the back-up device and reason for your choice.

Zip drives

Special high capacity floppy disks can be used in special drives called **zip drives** to back-up hard drives. These **floppies** are slightly larger and twice as thick as normal floppies. They are also used to transfer large files between machines.

CD-ROMs/compact disks

CD-ROMs are also known as **optical disks** and work in the same way as **compact disks** used to store and play music. Data is stored **digitally**, by changing the way the surface reflects a low energy laser beam. The light is reflected differently according to whether the bit (see 1.3) stored is a 1 or a 0. A low intensity beam is used to read the data but a higher intensity beam is needed to write the data onto the disk.

Optical disks have a huge capacity because data can be packed very closely. They are ideal for holding graphics that require large amounts of **storage space**, such as **clip art** that can be incorporated into documents. They can also hold entire encyclopaedias, photographs and all sorts of reference material. Optical disks are read in the **CD drive** that forms a standard part of most computer systems. They are more reliable than floppy disks and, because of their great capacity and ease of access, software can be run direct from them without the need to transfer it to the **hard drive** of a **processing unit**.

If software is held on an optical disk, it does not need to be copied on to another storage medium for back-up purposes.

> **KEY POINT**
>
> Once the surface of a basic optical disk has been altered to store data, it cannot be changed so that, although these disks can be read many times, they can be written only once. Data cannot be altered, nor can new data be added. However, disks that can be written by the user (CD-R), and disks that can be written and read many times over (CD-RW) are available also.

CD-R

CD-ROMs are faster than floppy disks.

These are recordable **optical disks**. A user can put a blank disk into the CD-R drive and use it to save data or programs. The disk has the same **high capacity** as a CD-ROM. Write access is not as fast as to a hard disk, but for many uses, this is not critical.

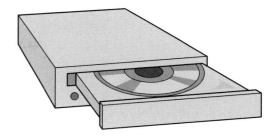

Read/Write CD-ROM drive

CD-R disks are useful for making back-up copies of data files for archiving. There is no need to re-write the disks.

The basic **CD-R** disk can be written only once. It contains a layer of special dye covered by a very thin layer of gold. This in turn is covered in a protective plastic coating. When the data is written to the disk, a laser beam is directed on to the dye. The dye absorbs the light and its structure is changed. As a result, the shape of the gold layer changes at this point so that it no longer reflects light when the disk is read. The new shape cannot be altered again. A more powerful laser beam is required to write a disk, and, because the beam that reads the disk is less powerful, it does not affect the dye and gold, so that the disk can be read many times.

CD-RW

Make sure you understand the difference between the two types of CD. One can only be written to once (CD-R), the other many times (CD-RW).

CD-RW disks can be written, erased and rewritten many times. They contain a chemical that changes between reflective and non-reflective forms when heated by a high energy laser beam. They are more expensive than **CD-R** disks and can be used only in a suitable drive.

Magnetic tape

Magnetic tape used to be a popular medium for backing storage, but is becoming less popular as disks and CDs are developed further. This is largely because of the type of access to data that the different storage media offer.

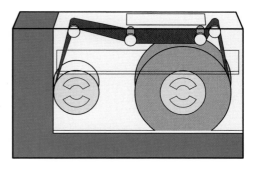

Magnetic tape backup

An example of a situation where magnetic tape might still be used would be in processing payments for a large company. Everyone working for the company will have to be paid, so all records will need to be processed. The serial access aspect of magnetic tape will therefore not be a limitation and it will be convenient for the company to carry out all the wages processing in one huge batch.

Disks and CDs provide **direct access** storage. In other words, any data item on them can be accessed directly without the need to read other data first. Magnetic tape provides **serial access**. All the data before the required item must be read before the required item can be accessed.

Magnetic tape remains useful for keeping back-up copies of data. Tape streamers are devices that hold a tape cartridge which can be used to back up all the data held on a hard disk. (Standard floppy disks would not be suitable for this purpose because their capacity is not great enough.)

Some large computer systems still use large spools of **reel-to-reel** tape to hold large amounts of **data** in **storage**. The reels fit into large tape drives.

A block is the amount of data that can be read or written at one time. The interblock gaps allow for starting and stopping the tape in the drive.

In some contexts, **magnetic** tape on large spools has been replaced by tape in **cartridges** that look like audio cassettes, only larger. On all magnetic

tape, data is organised into **blocks**, with interblock gaps between it. A block can often hold several records and there will be end-of-record markers between the records.

DVD

Some DVDs can store
the equivalent of 26
CD-ROMs.

Digital versatile disks look like **CD-ROMs** and can be used to store quantities of data in the same way. Their capacity is considerably greater than CD-ROMs. For example, a package of applications software stored on six or seven CD-ROMs could be stored on a single **DVD**. DVDs can be used to store applications software, multi-media programs and full-length films.

DVDs are read in DVD drives, and the most recent generation of DVDs can also be written by the user so that they can be used in much the same way as a hard disk.

DVDs used to store films produce much better quality pictures and sound than standard video tape. A film stored on DVD can even offer the viewer a choice of language in which the film can be played back.

PROGRESS CHECK

1. Explain the function of a storage device.
2. What is the purpose of memory in a computer system?
3. Explain the difference between volatile and non-volatile memory.

1. A medium that can be used to store data before or after processing. Data may be stored within the central processing unit of a computer, in main store memory, or it may be held outside the central processing unit, in various types of backing stores.
2. Memory is used to hold operating system programs and applications programs. It can hold data that has been input, provide a working area to store data that is currently being processed and hold output data before it is sent to an output device.
3. Any data that is held in volatile memory is lost when power is switched off. Data held in non-volatile memory is saved, even when there is no power connection.

Sample GCSE questions

1

```
A  →  B  →  C
      ↓↑
      D
```

> Look at the arrows. They hold the key to getting the question correct; a printer is an output device, mouse an input device, disk drive a read and write device.

(a) The block diagram represents the parts of a computer system.

Which parts represent:
(i)	A printer	*C*	**[1]**
(ii)	A mouse or keyboard	*A*	**[1]**
(iii)	A disk drive	*D*	**[1]**

(b) Describe the purpose of B.

B represents the processor and main storage unit. **[2]**

(c) If you bought an encyclopaedia in computerised form, what would it most likely be stored on and why?

A CD-ROM as it will store large amounts of read only data. This would be the most appropriate form of data storage as the user needs to read it but not write to it. **[3]**

> Think about size, data holding capacity and use. Some exam questions will ask you to compare different types of storage media including books.

(d) State the type of device that would be used to collect data in a remote computer controlled system.

A sensor **[1]**

2 Fashion Store is a high street shop selling clothing.

(a) Give the name of TWO input devices that must be part of the shop's work station.

Input device one	*Keyboard*	**[1]**
Input device two	*Scanner*	**[1]**

(b) Give the name of TWO output devices that must be part of the shop's system.

Output device one	*Screen*	**[1]**
Output device two	*Printer*	**[1]**

(c) Describe the benefit to Fashion Store of using bar codes.

Bar codes can be read very quickly using a bar code reader/scanner. Queues at the checkout are kept shorter and there is less chance of a mistake being made by incorrect data entry. **[4]**

> Think about a supermarket or shop. Who enters the data? How much time do they have? How can you ensure accuracy and speed?

Sample GCSE questions

3 Fashion Store intends to produce a brochure showing five fashion garments. Two of the garments are shown in existing conventional photographs; the other three are to be modelled by customers.

(a) Describe input devices the store should use to capture the existing photographs in digital format.

Scanner **[1]**

(b) Describe the process of capturing digital images of the models wearing the other three garments.

Digital photographs would be taken and transferred into the computer via a cable or digital film reader. **[3]**

(c) What type of printer could be used to produce a single copy of the leaflet? Give a reason for your choice.

Printer: *Ink-jet or laser* **[1]**

Reason: *Good colour reproduction, relatively low cost, quiet.* **[2]**

> *The fact that the shop wants a single copy helps you to answer this question.*

(d) State why digital colour pictures used in magazines are usually stored on CD-ROM or Zip disks rather than conventional floppy disks.

Pictures take up a large amount of memory and zip disks and CD-ROMs hold more digital data than floppy disks. **[2]**

> *Think about size of digital colour pictures. Some are too large for a conventional floppy disk.*

4 Most computers include a CD-ROM drive, floppy disk and hard drive. Some now have read-writers and Zip disks.

(a) Tick the box in the table to give the best description of the devices shown. **[9]**

	Floppy disk	Hard disk	CD-ROM	Zip disk	CD writer and read-write disk
Is the cheapest	✔				
Retrieves data the fastest		✔			
Is not portable		✔			
Can only be written to once			✔		
Holds large amounts of data		✔	✔	✔	✔
Is like a floppy disk but holds more data				✔	

> *Remember to tick ALL the boxes that apply.*

(b) Describe what you must do to a floppy disk before you can use it.

It must be formatted to enable the magnetic media to store data. **[2]**

Sample GCSE questions

5   Name the objects shown below and for each object state whether it is an input, output or storage item.

> Exam papers will use standard pictures. The pictures may, therefore, differ from the equipment you are used to using. Look for obvious clues.

Printer (output),   Scanner (input),   Keyboard (input),

CD-ROM (storage), floppy disk (storage).   **[5]**

6   Give two advantages and one disadvantage of using a CD-ROM encyclopaedia as opposed to a paper-based encyclopaedia.

Example answers:

Advantages: Quicker to access information you want; can contain video and sound files; usually has search facilities. Disadvantages: You need a computer and to know how to use the system; some religious beliefs do not allow the use of computers.   **[3]**

7   Compare the advantages and disadvantages of the following alternative ways of capturing pictures for use in the school magazine:

- scanner
- clip-art
- digital camera
- drawing the pictures yourself in a drawing package

Example answers:

Scanner - can copy any material from a range of sources, e.g. books, photos, magazines; fairly quick and easy to use. Disadvantages: cost of scanner; very dependent upon computer memory; could be problems with copyright.

Clip-art - copyright free when printed; easily available; very quick. Disadvantages: exact picture you want may not be available; publication could look just like everyone else's.

Digital camera - pictures copyright free because you have taken them; you can take pictures of exactly what you want. Disadvantages: cost of camera; transferring images from camera to computer can be difficult; you need to be a good photographer.

Drawing the pictures yourself in a drawing package - you will get exactly what you want; most computers have appropriate software already installed; relatively low cost; copyright free. Disadvantages: you have to be skilled at drawing; takes a long time to draw image.   **[16]**

Exam practice questions

1   What forms can a computer take? Describe typical uses of your examples.

....

....

....

....

....

....

.... **[8]**

2   What are the advantages or disadvantages of digital cameras as input devices?

....

....

....

....

....

....

.... **[8]**

3   What are the advantages or disadvantages of sound recognition software for inputting data?

....

....

....

....

.... **[6]**

4   Describe the main features of ROM and RAM.

....

....

....

....

.... **[6]**

Exam practice questions

5 List the main types of backing stores, with their uses.

....

....

....

....

....

.... **[6]**

6 What are the advantages or disadvantages of audible output devices?

....

....

....

....

....

.... **[6]**

Software

The following topics are covered in this chapter:

- **3.1 Operating environment and systems tasks**
- **3.2 Communicating with the operating system**
- **3.3 Applications software**

3.1 Operating environment and systems tasks

LEARNING SUMMARY

After completing this section you should be able to:

- *explain what is meant by the term operating environment*
- *explain the term software, and the difference between systems software and applications software*
- *describe the three main types of user interface: command-driven, menu-driven and graphical user interface*
- *describe the typical functions of an operating system*

The operating environment

OCR A   OCR B
EDEXCEL
AQA A   AQA B
NICCEA
WJEC

The term **operating environment** refers to the interaction of an **information system**, typically a computer system, with the user. There must be a means of communication between the system and the user (the **user interface**), and between the system hardware and the software.

Software is the general term used to describe all of the programs that can be run on computer hardware.

Software can be divided into:

- **systems software**, that controls computer operating systems, and
- **applications software**, that covers the range of user related programs that can be run

The **user interface** is also known as the **human computer interface** (**HCI**). It provides the means of communication between the user, or users, and the information system. Ideally, it should be as easy to use as possible, so that users do not need to study detailed instructions before they switch on the system.

> To answer exam questions you must understand the differences between these three interfaces and remember the terms used to describe them.

The **interface** consists of the **cursors**, **prompts**, **icons**, **menus**, etc, that enable the user to achieve a desired task by means of the **information system**. Prompts can be visual or audible.

User interfaces can be described as either:

- command-driven
- menu-driven, or
- **graphical** (called a GUI – graphical user interface)

Command-driven interface

This method was used in early computer systems to communicate with the **operating system** [see page 48]. With a command-driven interface, the user must enter a command in order to get something done. The command is usually typed on a keyboard. Typically, it is in an abbreviated form, and must be entered correctly (including any punctuation and spaces) or the desired end result will not be achieved.

KEY POINT

Commands vary with different software and for this reason, and because they may not be easy to remember, command-driven interfaces are not very popular with many users. For those users, however, who find commands easy to memorise and use them frequently, this type of interface provides fast access to the functions of the system.

Menu-driven interface

In this type of interface, system functions are accessed through lists of commands or options that appear on the screen. A selection is made by using a **mouse** or **touch sensitive pad**, or via a **keyboard**. The method is easier to use than a command-driven interface.

KEY POINT

Menus are intended to be user-friendly in that the user does not necessarily have to study a manual before being able to access the system. Aspects of both Windows and Apple Macintosh programs are menu-driven.

Graphical user interface (GUI)

GUI is said to make use of a WIMP environment. This stands for Windows, Icons, Menus and Pointers, each of which are typical features of a GUI.

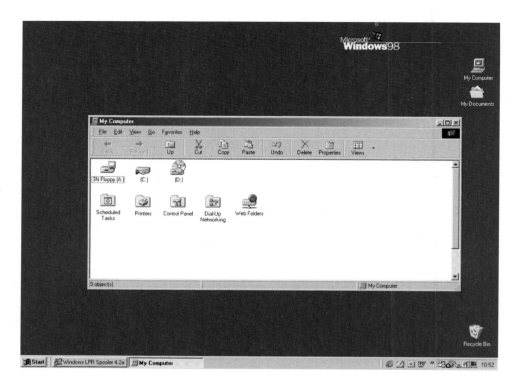

This is probably the most accessible type of **interface**, where system functions are accessed by selecting pictures (**icons**) and items from **pull-down menus**. The icons and menu items are intended to be self-explanatory although, as they differ from software to software, some initial user guidance often remains necessary. Windows and Apple Macintosh programs use a graphical user interface.

Operating system

OCR A **OCR B**
EDEXCEL
AQA A **AQA B**
WJEC

The means of communication between user, system hardware and software is called the **operating system**. Via the user **interface**, the user indicates what he or she wishes to do, and the operating system provides the routines that are needed to allow the **hardware** to interact with **applications software**.

KEY POINT

The operating system is a complex program that controls the entire operation of the computer. Examples of four commonly used operating systems are:
- LINUX – a unique system in that it was conceived by one computer expert but developed with input from computer users throughout the world.
- UNIX – written in computer language C; a system that is often found on larger systems like minicomputers and mainframes as it is a multi-user, multi-tasking system.
- Microsoft Windows 95/98 – a system that is widely used on PCs in businesses, schools and homes.
- Microsoft Windows NT/Windows 2000 – a more complex, multi-tasking system than 95/98; widely used in network environments.

You should remember the names of some of the more popular operating systems.

The following are typical functions of an operating system:
- It allocates a '**time slot**' with the processor for each job that needs to be processed.
- It allocates **memory** for storing programs and data so that when data is needed, it can be found easily. New data is not put in areas of memory that have already been allocated.

The system must be able to differentiate between input devices such as keyboard or mouse and handle the data accordingly, and it must do the same for output devices such as printer or speaker. Data must be sent to the correct output device.

You do not need to know how an operating system functions in terms of programming, but you do need to understand the main functions of an operating system.

- It ensures that jobs with different **priorities** are dealt with in the correct order.
- The system takes care of **data storage** in the computer system's memory. It must keep track of what space is available as well as what has already been allocated, to make the best possible use of memory space.
- It has routines for **handling input** and **output** operations.
- It accepts commands and data from the user via input devices, interprets commands, transfers data to memory, retrieves data from memory and sends it to output devices.
- The system looks after transfers of data between the backing store and memory. If a file has to be read from disk, operating system routines must first locate the file, using a specific search path. The file is then opened and blocks of data transferred. Where a file is being written to disk for backing storage, the operating system builds up blocks of data until they are ready to transfer. As each block is ready, it is sent to the disk drive which writes it on to the disk.
- The operating system also manages **system security**. Many systems allocate certain rights to particular users. A user can access a function only by entering a unique password.

Methods of operation

OCR A OCR B
EDEXCEL
AQA A AQA B
WJEC

Computers are designed to operate in a number of different ways, or **modes**. These include:

- **Single program mode**.
The computer runs with just one program at a time, with one user.

- **Multi-tasking mode**/**multi-program mode**.
The computer runs with two or more programs at a time, with one user. The operating system makes sure that the **resources** of the computer, including **processor time**, are shared between the programs running.

You will need to understand what type of system is best suited to what type of application. For example a school network would need a multi-processor server. A small office of say eight computers could run in multi-user mode with a single processor in the server.

- **Multi-user mode**.
Several users are able to use the same system together. The operating system allocates each user a **share** of processor time. This is called a **time slice**.

- **Multi-processor mode**.
In larger systems, there will be more than one **processor**. The operating system allows the different processors to operate together and utilise the same memory.

- See also **batch mode** and **real-time processing** (page 83).

System utilities

OCR A OCR B
EDEXCEL
AQA A AQA B
WJEC

In addition to the operating system itself, a computer system is supplied with a range of **system utility programs**. These are designed to carry out certain routine functions like formatting floppy disks. They can also check disks for damaged areas, called **bad sectors**, that cannot store data. Utilities can copy files from one disk to another, sort files and print them.

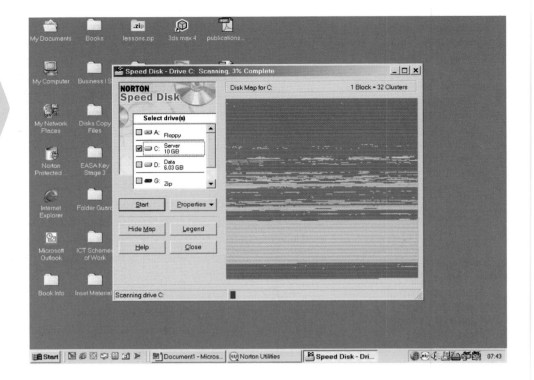

The utilities provided with the operating system can also be supplemented by other purchasable utilities to speed up or tune up the operating system.

KEY POINT

The operating system is not always able to cope with new devices that are added. For example, if a new, sophisticated printer or a scanner is added to the system, extra software will have to be installed to make the device work. This kind of software is called a device driver. Once it has been installed on a hard disk, data going to the printer or coming from the scanner will first be processed by the device driver before moving on through the system.

PROGRESS CHECK

1. Explain what is meant by the term operating environment.
2. Explain the term software, and the difference between systems software and applications software.
3. List the four main modes in which a computer might be operating, and state which mode allows several users to use the same system.

1. It refers to the area of contact between an information system, typically a computer system, and the human user.
2. The word used to describe all the programs that run on a computer. Systems software controls how the computer and peripherals work, and applications software provides user-related functions such as desktop publishing, Web design, or database creation and management.
3. Single program mode, multi-tasking mode, multi-user mode and multi-processor mode. Multi-user mode allows several people to use the same system, with a time slice each.

3.2 Communicating with the operating system

LEARNING SUMMARY

After completing this section you should be able to:

● *describe how a user can employ system commands to communicate with an operating system*
● *describe the main types of programming languages, dividing them into low-level languages and high-level languages*
● *explain the term machine code*
● *describe the function of assemblers, interpreters and compilers*

Interpretation of commands

EDEXCEL

Operating systems have their own **commands** and a user can employ system commands to investigate the system, for example to find out how much **memory** is available, or to find out what is on a particular disk. To achieve this, the user has to display the **disk directory**, which appears in a tree format with many branches.

> The name given to this is a directory tree.

The branches represent **subdirectories** and these in turn can have **smaller branches**, further **subdirectories**.

Operating system commands allow a user to create and remove **subdirectories** so that disk storage can be organised in a useful way. To enable the user to locate an item of data quickly, without having to look through each directory, with its **subdirectories**, he or she can set up a **search path** to enable the operating system to indicate a particular subdirectory straight away. A subdirectory called invitations might be accessed using the following path:

D:\windows\msapps\invitations

> A user can put together batches of commands to carry out particular tasks.

Batch files are often produced when new software is installed. A **batch file** is a group of commands that can be saved with a name, which can then be used like a **system command** to make the new software load.

Programming languages

OCR A **OCR B**
EDEXCEL
AQA A **AQA B**
WJEC

Program commands must be converted into **machine code** (or language) before the computer can actually understand them.

> This code is binary, consisting of 1s and 0s, and is the language directly understood by the machine.

KEY POINT

Machine code is often machine specific. This means that one computer's machine code will not be understood by a different type of computer. Commands written in machine code produce rapid results because they do not have to be translated into another language and, for this reason, many games and simulation programs are written in machine code.

Assembly language

OCR A   OCR B
EDEXCEL
AQA A   AQA B
WJEC

Machine code and assembly language are known as low-level languages.

KEY POINT The term low-level means that they are easy for the computer to understand, but more difficult for the programmer.

An assembly language uses simple instructions like ADD or SUB. Programmers may use it in preference to machine code because it is easier for the programmer. It is also easier to debug assembly language. This means removing any mistakes from it. However, once a program has been written in assembly language, it must be translated into machine code by software called an assembler before the computer can understand it. This makes it slightly slower.

High-level language

OCR A   OCR B
EDEXCEL
AQA A   AQA B
WJEC

High-level programming languages have been developed with the programmer in mind. Commands are written in a form that resembles English, which makes programming easier.

> BASIC is one example of a high-level language and includes commands such as GOTO, PRINT and READ.

KEY POINT Another advantage of high-level languages is that they are not machine specific. Once a program has been written, it can be used on various types of computer with little alteration.

Error correction and testing is also straightforward with high-level languages.

> You do not need to be familiar with all these languages but you should be aware that they exist.

KEY POINT Examples of high-level languages that have been developed for specific programming purposes are:
- BASIC – mainly used as a teaching language
- C++ – used for graphics and for development of commercial software
- COBOL – used for business data processing because it offers excellent file handling
- FORTRAN – used in scientific programs
- HTML (hypertext markup language) – used to create websites
- JAVA – used to write software that will search for things on Internet
- LOGO – used to teach children about programming and using computers

All high-level languages must be translated into machine code by specialised systems software before the computer can understand them. Assemblers convert low-level assembly language, and compilers and interpreters convert high-level languages. Compilers and interpreters work in different ways:

- An interpreter takes each instruction in turn, converts it to machine code, then carries it out. If the document needs to be read again at a later date, the same process has to be repeated.
- A compiler converts the whole of a program written in a high-level language (called the source code) into machine code in one go. The conversion, now in machine code (called the object code) can be written to a disk for repeated use. If a program needs to be altered at a later date, the source code can be changed and the program recompiled.

PROGRESS CHECK

1. How can a user employ system commands to communicate with an operating system?
2. What are assemblers, compilers and interpreters used for?
3. What are the main differences between low-level programming languages and high-level programming languages?

1. Operating systems have their own typical commands and a user can use these commands to investigate the system, for example to find out what is on a particular disk. On most systems, files are organised into directories, which can have subdirectories, and these can be displayed in a tree format. The user can access the tree to find out what is in a particular subdirectory.
2. They are packages of specialised software used to convert low or high-level programming languages into machine code so that a computer can act on them.
3. Low-level programming languages are more accessible to the computer, but more difficult for programmers to use. High-level programming languages have been developed to make the programmer's task easier. Commands are written in a form that resembles English, making programming more straightforward. High-level languages are not machine specific and checking for errors is relatively simple.

3.3 *Applications software*

LEARNING SUMMARY

After completing this section you should be able to:

- *describe the three main types of applications software*
- *discuss the characteristics, and typical applications of the following types of software: database creation and management, spreadsheet creation and management, word processing, desk top publishing and other presentations, graphics packages, Web design, modelling and simulation, data logging and control*
- *develop a set of criteria to evaluate a software package*

Modern PCs have to have enormous processing power to cope with operating systems such as windows.

Applications software is designed to carry out **user-related** tasks. Some applications software has to be used within a particular **operating system**.

There are three main general types of **applications software**, as described below:

Applications packages, including integrated software

OCR A **OCR B**
EDEXCEL
AQA A **AQA B**
NICCEA
WJEC

Sometimes you could use different packages to achieve similar results. When asked to name a software package in an exam question, describe the functional characteristics that make it suitable.

An applications package is an item of software that has been designed to perform a specific function in terms of outcome, or for use within one particular industry.

Examples of specific functions are **word processing**, **spreadsheet** creation and management or **database** creation and management.

Integrated software consists of a matching collection of applications packages that are designed to be bought and used as a set. An integrated package is likely to include software for

A disadvantage of integrated packages is that they may be very strong in one particular area, such as spreadsheets, but relatively weak in another, such as graphics. If a user wants one particular function that is going to be used very extensively, it remains better to shop around and find a separate, specialised package.

word processing, spreadsheets, databases and graphics and may offer other features also.

KEY POINT

Advantages of integrated software over separate packages
- integrated software is normally less expensive to buy
- commands are normally common throughout the package, which makes them more user friendly
- moving data from one program to another within the integrated package is normally simpler than between separate packages

Tailor-made software

OCR A   OCR B
EDEXCEL
AQA A   AQA B
WJEC

Where there is a particular requirement, a company may employ its own experts to write **in-house software**, or it may employ a **software house** to write specialised software on its behalf. Such software is very expensive and is used only in companies with large computer departments, or where no suitable ready-written applications packages are available.

An example of a customised software situation is the traffic control department of a county council. At each road junction controlled by traffic lights there is a control box that controls all of the traffic lights and any pedestrian crossings at the junction. The program for each junction is individually written at the traffic control office to meet the characteristics and requirements of the particular junction. No two junctions are the same.

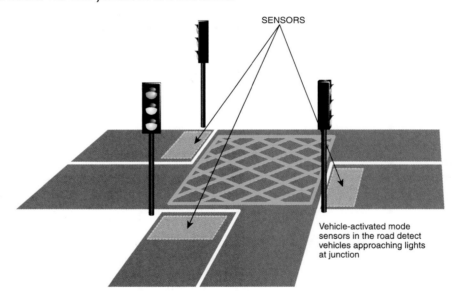

SENSORS

Vehicle-activated mode sensors in the road detect vehicles approaching lights at junction

General purpose packages

OCR A   OCR B
EDEXCEL
AQA A   AQA B
NICCEA
WJEC

A lot of ready-written applications software is not specific to a particular type of business. Some **database packages**, for example, can be used to develop tailor-made software. **General purpose** packages are very popular because their documentation (manuals, tutorials, etc) is usually excellent, programs are well tested, and they are inexpensive.

General purpose software is sometimes called content free software.

Macro programs

Programs that are used to automate actions in applications software are called **macros**. Some macro programs are produced using automated routines called **wizards**.

Macros can be used to automate a variety of user actions including:

- replace multiple key strokes
- insert graphics, text, tables, lines and borders
- adjust the page layout (margins, columns, headers, footers)
- call or create a new template
- modify application software configuration (set options, customise)

Creating templates

Templates are used to avoid repeating work every time you create a document. Most documents have parts that are always the same. For example, a letter template may contain:

- a page layout
- the logo of the company
- a date field
- part of a reference (Our Ref GB/)
- the opening greeting (Dear)
- a graphic image of a closing signature

Templates help users to work more efficiently and save them having to do the same work repeatedly.

Database creation and management

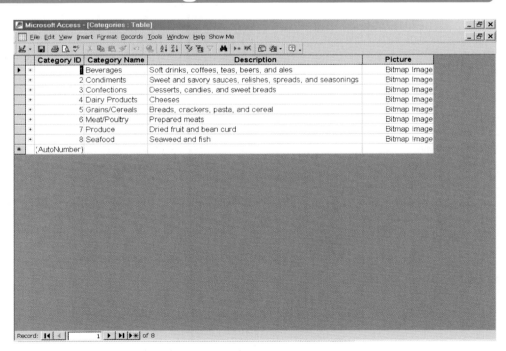

> **KEY POINT**
> A database program allows the user to handle files, keep records in an organised way, and retrieve information from these records.

There are two main types of database; a **flat file database** and a **relational database**.

Flat file databases

In a **flat file database** all the data is stored in a **single file** and the **sorting**, **searching** and **printing** of reports is all done in this single file.

Flat file databases are:

- easy to use
- suitable for small amounts of data

Relational databases

In relational databases, the tables of data exist **independently** from the programs that may use them. Relational databases use **database management systems** (**DBMS**) to **link** independent files together. Sometimes different users will have access to different data stored.

Some users will not be given permission to look at all the data.

> Sometimes examiners ask for the differences between flat and relational databases.

Table one

Customer number	Customer name	Postcode	Tel

Relationship between tables

Database management system

Table two

Order number	Customer number	Date	Number	Cost

> Examples of use: to sort, store, search and retrieve information.

> **KEY POINT**
> The characteristics of a database program are that:
> - Data is stored in the form of records. For example, if the database is about people, each record would contain all the data relating to one individual.
> - The user can define how records will be organised by choosing the number of fields and their names, the size of each field and type of data it will hold, the way records are displayed on the screen. (A field is an area of a record reserved for one particular type of data item. Each field contains one data item.)
> - The program provides facilities to sort data into different levels of importance.
> - It provides facilities for information retrieval. It can produce lists of all records that meet certain criteria, and it can calculate statistics for groups of records.
> - It can combine results into a report.

The sort, search and logical conditions used in a database are:

- sort ascending
- sort descending
- is equal to (=)
- is less than (<)
- is greater than (>)
- is less than or equal to (<=)
- is greater than or equal to (>=)
- is not equal to (<>)
- AND
- OR
- NOT

It is often necessary to use sort routines that make use of more than one field. Often it is necessary to make use of a primary and secondary sort field. An example is the telephone directory. This has an alphabetical list of names where 'last name' is the primary sort field and 'first name' is the secondary sort field. In this way Alan Cushing comes before Steven Cushing.

Sometimes we need to search for information using two criteria. One example of this would be to search for all **part-time** employees over **60** years of age. This type of search uses the logic condition **AND**. The search would be specified as follows:

Status = part-time AND Age > 60 years

Searches of this kind are called complex searches because they use two or more criteria.

To store information in computers you often need to classify and format the information in records and tables in more detail. Common database classifications are:

- text
- number (integer)
- number (decimal)
- currency
- date
- time
- formula
- logical (true or false value)

Each type of database has different ways of finding the information that is needed.

Three types of computer databases are:

- hypertext databases
- record-structured databases
- spreadsheet (number-structured) databases

Hypertext databases

OCR A OCR B
EDEXCEL
AQA A AQA B
NICCEA

Hypertext databases are pages of information with highlighted items of text or graphics. The highlighted items are linked to other pages or sections of information. Pointing at, or clicking on a highlighted item reveals more information about it. Internet pages, CD-ROM encyclopaedia pages and 'Help' facilities in software often use this method.

Record-structured databases

OCR A   OCR B

EDEXCEL

AQA A   AQA B

NICCEA

WJEC

Key Skills

Record-structured databases are usually rows of information in the form of a table. Each row is a record. Records could be people's names and addresses, information about a hotel in a travel database or flights and destinations in an airport. Many record-structured databases make use of several tables that are related to form one information system.

Organisations use a great deal of record-structured information.

- directory – name, telephone no., address
- patient record – name, diagnosis, date
- orders – item, quantity, price, total
- products – name, size, colour, price
- sports results – team, date, score
- houses for sale – address, bedrooms, price

Typical applications of databases are:

- creating and maintaining personal lists such as:
  - details of customers' names, addresses and accounts
  - details of patients names, addresses and medical or dental records
- student or pupil records
- lists of suppliers to a company
- allowing access to large stores of information such as:
  - an encyclopaedia stored on CD
  - details of books currently in print, with authors, publishers and contents summaries
  - details of properties for sale
  - details of careers available with qualification requirements

**Example software:
Microsoft Access,
PinPoint, dBase.**

Terminology used when describing database software

You should understand and use the following specialist terminology:

AND	Boolean	condition	criteria
field	field type	file	flat file
form	form	index	integer
key	key field	list	NOT
OR	query	record	relational
report	sort	string	subset
table	validation	view	

Spreadsheet databases – creation and management

OCR A   OCR B

EDEXCEL

AQA A   AQA B

WJEC

Key Skills

Spreadsheet software allows **data** and **information** to be displayed and managed in a **table format**.

Spreadsheets are really number-structured databases. They hold numerical data in cells that are laid out in rows and columns. One example is wages for staff that would include hours worked, pay rates and tax. Another example is the cost, sale price and profit of selling products. Companies use spreadsheets to calculate results such as totals and to produce graphs of the results. They also use spreadsheets to calculate or forecast results from given information.

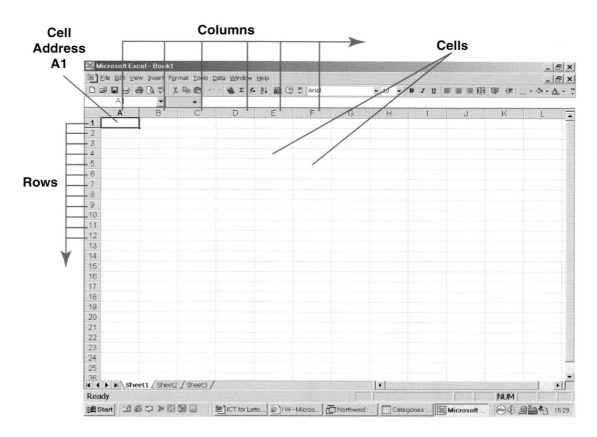

Cell Address A1

Columns

Cells

Rows

A spreadsheet table is divided into **rows** and **columns** of individual boxes called **cells**. A spreadsheet allows calculations to be carried out on cells or groups of cells, both within individual spreadsheets, or across **linked** spreadsheets.

KEY POINT

The characteristics of a spreadsheet program are:
- the user can enter a number, formula or text into any cell
- a formula can allow calculations to be carried out in other cells
- formulae and other data can be copied into groups of cells
- a variety of operations can be carried out on rows or columns. These might include functions such as auto-fill, where the spreadsheet automatically enters data such as months of the year or days of the week. It can start a table with a certain value and increase the value in subsequent cells in measured amounts, for example displaying 0 to 100 in steps of 5 each
- a spreadsheet allows the creation of macros. These are series of commands created by the user that the spreadsheet will perform automatically
- basic functions relating to appearance of the display, similar to those of a word processor. Examples are text formatting, creation of borders, use of colour and spell checking

Typical applications of spreadsheets are:

- displaying, calculating and managing accounts and other financial information

- performing calculations on data collected in experiments and surveys

- producing data from which graphs can be drawn, for example to calculate average temperature for a graph of weather data, or to solve a mathematical equation

Typical industrial uses of a spreadsheet are:

- income and expenditure
- sales forecasting
- staff hours, rates of pay and tax
- mortgage payments and interest rates
- material and quantities for jobs
- number statistics

Terminology used when describing spreadsheet software

You should understand and use the following specialist terminology:

absolute reference	border	cell	reference
column	copy	data	embedding
fill	footer	formats	formula
functions	gridlines	header	label
label	legend	link	lock/unlock
macro	operator	paste	paste special
preview	range	relative reference	replicate
row	run	scrolling	sort
text	tool bar	window	

Word processing

OCR A   OCR B
EDEXCEL
AQA A   AQA B
NICCEA
WJEC
Key Skills

Example uses:
letters, memos,
books, essays.

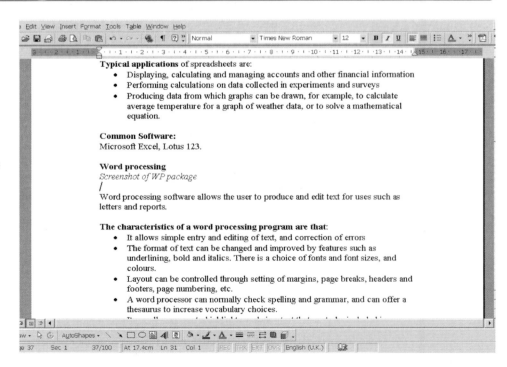

Word processing software allows the user to produce and **edit text** for uses such as letters and reports.

> **KEY POINT**
>
> **The characteristics of a word processing program are that:**
> - it allows simple entry and editing of text, and correction of errors
> - the format of text can be changed and improved by features such as underlining, bold and italics. There is a choice of fonts and font sizes, and colours
> - layout can be controlled through setting of margins, page breaks, headers and footers, page numbering, etc
> - a word processor can normally check spelling and grammar, and can offer a thesaurus to increase vocabulary choices
> - it can allow a user to highlight words in a text that are to be included in an index, and can then create the index
> - it can find specific words in a text and replace them if required to do so
> - it provides facilities for printing and addressing sets of printed letters or memos

Typical applications of word processors are:

- writing letters, memos, reports, lists and other text documents in an office or home environment

Example Software: Microsoft Word, WordPerfect.

- producing the text of books and articles. Although the design and completion of a book or magazine may be carried out using desktop publishing software, the text is still often written in a word processing package

- producing sets of similar letters, with personalised details, to be sent to numbers of people. An example would be when a company sends out a mailshot to advertise a new product. This technique is called mail merging. A list of letter recipients is compiled, either by the word processor, or by importing data from a database, a standard letter is created, and the personalised data inserted into blanks in each letter.

Accuracy and readability

Inaccuracy can mislead and annoy readers. Spell-checkers are included with most word processing software and often with other software. They help the user to correct spelling and some other mistakes. Spell-checkers can detect:

- words spelt incorrectly
- repeated words (for example, 'and and')

Sometimes a spell-checker will suggest that a word is incorrect when the user knows it is correct. This often happens with proper names, for example 'GCSE', or 'Peter'.

Users can add these words to a computer's user dictionary to resolve the problem. Using a spell-checker will not find all errors. It will not correct 'capitol' for 'capital' or 'there' for 'their' or 'to' for 'too'.

Alongside spell-checkers most word processors have grammar-checkers. These are used to:

- make sure sentences have a subject and a verb that agree
- find out the level of reading difficulty
- check that writing is mostly in a certain style, for example in the active voice
- detect sentences ending with two full-stops
- detect missing capital letters at the beginning of sentences

Terminology used when describing word processing software

You should understand and use the following specialist terminology:

bold	bullet	clip art	copy
crop	cut	font	footer
format	header	indent	insert
italic	justification	link	menu
OCR	orphan	outline	overtype
page layout	paste	preview	proportional
roman	ruler	sans serif	scrolling
search	serif	subscript	superscript
template	thesaurus	toolbar	typeface

Desktop publishing and other presentation software

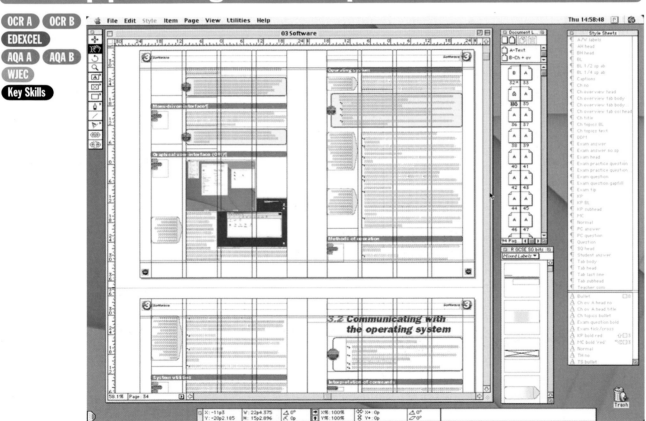

Desktop publishing software allows the user to produce **text** and **pictures** and organise them into pages. It produces work that is of a quality good enough for publication.

Presentation software can put together **text** and **pictures** in a similar way. The end result is usually a set of high quality slides, which can have a degree of **animation**, to be used in a presentation to an audience. The presentation is made via a computer screen, or for better effect, on a large screen via a **projector**.

The quality of this type of presentation can have a very positive effect on the image of the trainer or company using it. It can help to explain information that can be technical and complicated in an accessible way.

> **KEY POINT**
>
> **The characteristics of a desktop publishing or presentation program are that:**
> - the document is divided into pages, or slides, and these may in turn be divided into columns
> - the software offers word processing features, with a good range of fonts and other format options. Lines, boxes, bullets, borders and colour can be used to enhance effect
> - style sheets can be used to help make main text, headings and subheadings consistent. The master page and paragraph styles for a document can be saved as a template to ensure that each page or slide looks the same overall
> - there is a drawing capability
> - there are good facilities for importing word processor or other files. The software can import data from scanners and digital cameras and utilise this
> - there are good facilities for arranging text and pictures together in eye-catching ways, and changing their sizes. Pictures can also be cropped. This is the term for cutting off and discarding part of a picture that is not needed

Modern word processors can be used to publish documents. They often can be used to carry out most of the DTP functions. Commercially, professional DTP programmes produce higher quality and printer ready files.

Presentation software does not usually need to produce documents in as high a resolution as DTP software.

Typical applications of desktop publishing software are:

- to produce newspapers, newsletters, journals, magazines and books
- to produce reports, brochures and manuals
- to produce posters and advertisements
- to add pictures, logos, etc, to letters or other documents to make them look attractive

Typical **applications** of presentation software are:

- to launch new products
- to give a key note address to an audience

Example DTP software: Microsoft Publisher, Adobe PageMaker, Adobe InDesign. Presentation Software: Microsoft PowerPoint

Terminology used when describing DTP software

You should understand and use the following specialist terminology:

bold	bullet	clip art	copy
crop	cut	font	footer
format	header	indent	insert
italic	justification	link	menu
OCR	orphan	outline	overtype
page layout	paste	preview	proportional
roman	ruler	sans serif	scrolling
search	serif	subscript	superscript
template	thesaurus	toolbar	typeface

Graphics

OCR A   OCR B
EDEXCEL
AQA A   AQA B
WJEC

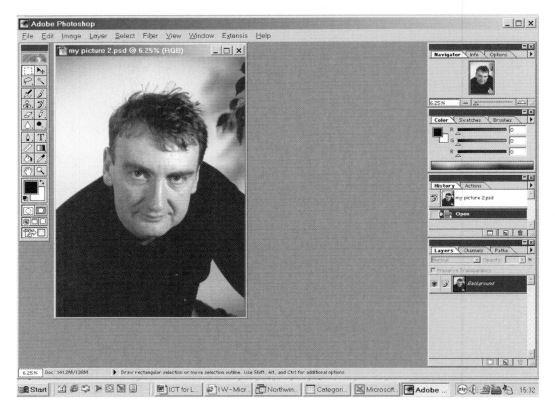

Software packages that produce **graphics** can be divided into four main types, according to their function:

● graphs and charts, sometimes called business graphics
● painting and drawing programs
● image manipulation programs
● Computer Aided Design (CAD) packages

Graphics files in general are of two main types. There are those that represent **images** as **vector graphics**, and those that present images as **bit maps**.

> You should understand the differences between bit maps and vector graphics.

Vector graphics

With **vector graphics**, lines are stored in the computer as **equations**. They are expressed in vector format so they have a starting point, a length and a direction.

> As well as being used in software for painting and drawing, vector graphics are used in CAD packages.

> **KEY POINT**
> Vector graphics are easy to change without any loss of resolution. When a vector graphics image is enlarged, the number of pixels used to make up the image increases in proportion, so the detail remains the same.

Bit map graphics

Bit map graphics are used in software designed to manipulate images. Such software is often used alongside a digital camera and can change and enhance pictures that have been taken.

> **KEY POINT**
>
> A bit map file represents each pixel on the screen as a single bit of information. If the pixel is in colour, additional bits will need to be stored. If the user wants to change a bit mapped image, the software has to alter it one pixel at a time. If the image is enlarged, the number of pixels stays the same and, as a result, the pixels move apart, making the image look grainy and less clear.

Business graphics programs

> **KEY POINT**
>
> The characteristics of a business graphics program are that:
> - it can import sets of data from a database or spreadsheet
> - it offers a choice of graphs including pie charts, bar charts of all kinds, line graphs and *x-y* or scatter graphs
> - it can label the graph, the axes and the data, as appropriate
> - it offers a range of colours and formats to enhance the presentation of graphs and charts

Typical applications of business graphics software are:
- to present statistics in a form that can be easily understood. For example, using a pie chart to show the different age groups of population in a town, or using a line graph to show how the price of petrol has increased over a number of years
- to sketch mathematical functions

Painting and drawing programs

> **KEY POINT**
>
> The characteristics of a painting and drawing program are that:
> - it offers good facilities for freehand drawing, with a wide choice of pens, brushes and drawing styles, and a wide range of colours and patterns
> - a range of standard shapes to include in pictures is provided
> - choices are made mainly with a mouse and icons
> - areas to be deleted, copied or moved can be marked out
> - there is a zoom facility to change individual pixels

> You will be expected to be able to choose the right program for a given situation.

Typical applications of painting and drawing software are:
- to produce pictures on the screen, providing a chance to be creative. The pictures can be printed
- to produce simple illustrations for use on documents

Terminology used when describing graphics software

You should understand and use the following specialist terminology:

bold	bullet	clipart	copy	sans serif
crop	cut	digitiser	flip	scanner
font	footer	format	freehand	scrolling
graphics tablet	header	hyphen	indent	search
insert	italic	justification	light pen	serif
link	menu	mirror	orphan	spray
outline	overtype	page layout	paste	template
pixel	plotter	preview	projector	thesaurus
proportional	roman	ruler	toolbar	typeface
vector image	window	wordwrap	zoom	

CAD programs

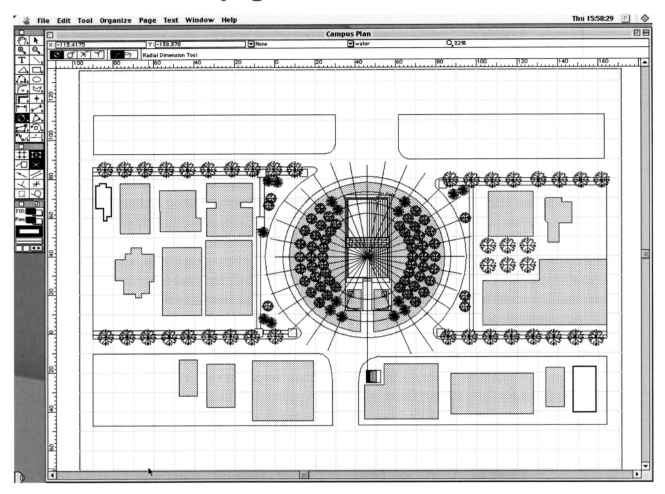

KEY POINT

The characteristics of a CAD program are that:
- It can generate very accurate drawings which can be reduced in size or enlarged without losing accuracy.
- Different types of line can be used for drawing.
- Images, including 3D images, can be manipulated on screen.
- The corners of shapes can be rounded automatically.
- Devices such as a grid on the screen, or a graphics digitiser [see page 22] can be used to ensure that input is as accurate as possible.

Example use: Design, scale drawing, systems design.

A CAD package has far more **standard** shapes than a simple drawing package. These can be used as basic tools for drawing.

Example software: AutoCAD, Fashion Studio

It can perform **calculations** on designs. For example, it can calculate the actual length of lines from a scale, and work out the areas of the shapes that have been drawn to scale. It can also carry out costings on a design.

Typical applications of a CAD program are:

- in architecture, to produce designs for buildings
- in traffic control, to produce detailed drawings of road junction layouts
- in engineering drawing of all kinds, for example to produce the exterior and interior designs for cars
- in any other industrial context where accurate drawings are required. For each application, a set of standard library shapes is available, for example electronic components for circuit diagrams
- fashion design

Clip art

OCR A   OCR B
EDEXCEL
AQA A   AQA B
WJEC
Key Skills

Clip art is the name given to **illustrations** that are **copyright-free** and intended for use in documents of all kinds, where the user does not want to draw something from scratch.

KEY POINT

The use of clip art can save time and help to produce a document with a more professional appearance. Disks containing clip art can be bought separately or as part of a DTP or graphics package. As many as one million images may be available in a clip art package.

Clip art illustrations can be added to all kinds of documents, from word processed documents, spreadsheets, desktop published documents to graphics.

You can buy CDs of clip art images. You should understand the importance of copyright and draw attention to its importance when discussing the use of images.

Web design

OCR A   OCR B
EDEXCEL
AQA A   AQA B
WJEC

Web sites can be professionally designed and created, or they can be designed and created by individuals working in a domestic setting. There are a number of software packages that are used to design and create web sites. See page 71.

Most word processors will save work in HTML for publishing on the web. Word processors are not as versatile as a web design program.

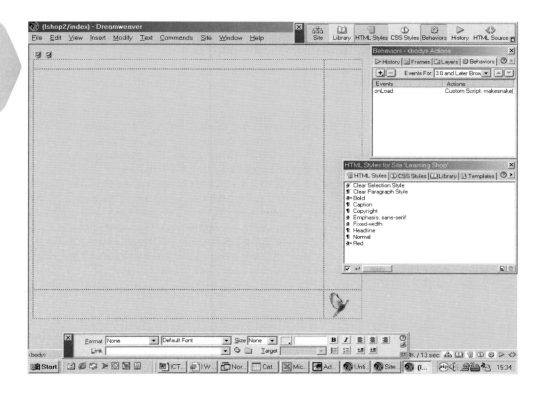

KEY POINT

The characteristic of a web design program is that:
● it usually helps the user to construct HTML code

Typical applications of a web program are:

- to produce a website for a school, company or home
- to design a user friendly interface for a computer game or software package

Terminology used when describing the Internet

You should understand and use the following specialist terminology:

ASCII	bookmark	bps	browser
CGI	cookies	demodulation	direct access
DNS	domain name	downloading	email
FTP	gopher	HTML	Hyperlink
hypertext	IRC	ISDN	ISP
mailing list	mirrored server	modem	netiquet
network	newsgroup	ping	PoP
PPP	protocol	search engine	SLIP
surfing	tags	TCP	transfer
Trojans	uploading	URL	UUENCODE
viruses	web page	web server	www
zip			

Modelling and simulation

OCR A   OCR B
EDEXCEL
AQA A   AQA B
WJEC

Modelling and simulation software is designed to allow the user to ask the question 'What if . . .?', given a particular set of circumstances. The software allows the creation of a computer model, which can be either a:

- mathematical model; or a
- simulation model

KEY POINT

The **characteristics** of a modelling or simulation program are that:
- **A computer model contains data and rules. The rules control the way the model works. They are instructions for carrying out calculations, or conditions when particular calculations should be carried out.**
- **The model can be of a situation or a process.**
- **It is much cheaper to set up a computer model than to build a whole system for testing. Simulation provides a relatively inexpensive way for games players to experience 'real' exciting situations.**
- **The user of a computer model can make changes quickly and easily to find out what happens if the situation changes.**
- **Tests or games can be repeated as often as the user wishes.**

Typical applications of modelling or simulation software are:

- Spreadsheet software is normally used for the mathematical model type. An example use would be for modelling financial situations. When preparing a new budget, the Chancellor of the Exchequer will use a mathematical model to look at the potential results of budget decisions, such as changing the amount the government spends on services such as education, or the health service, or of raising or cutting taxes in particular sectors.
- A company finance director will use a mathematical model in the same kind of way to assess, for example, the potential result of buying an expensive new piece of equipment.

LOGO

OCR A OCR B
EDEXCEL
AQA A AQA B

LOGO is an example of a **control program** that is widely used in school and college environments. It includes a set of **commands** to move a simple robot called a floor turtle around to produce patterns. It is ideal for learning some of the basics of control programming, using the following simple instructions: PEN DOWN, PEN UP, FORWARD, BACKWARD, LEFT, RIGHT and REPEAT.

> Some exam questions ask you to give simple instructions to a floor turtle or screen turtle to draw a simple shape.

KEY POINT

- For the Forward and Backward commands, a number of steps are added to tell the turtle how far to move. This can be in the form of time.
- For the Left and Right commands, a number of degrees is added in the same way.
- For Repeat, square brackets can follow the command to tell the turtle what to repeat. It can also be told how many times to repeat.

Movement of the **floor turtle** can be used to draw shapes on paper.

A screen image can be produced using a device called a screen turtle. Screen movement can be controlled with the same instructions that move the floor turtle. An arrow is used to show the direction of movement on the screen.

KEY POINT

A floor turtle needs the following:
- a wheel or wheels driven by stepper motors to enable it to move a precise distance in a particular direction
- a guide wheel or similar device driven by a stepper motor to enable it to turn through an exact number of degrees to face in another direction
- a writing device, usually a pen, that can be lowered so that the turtle can leave a written trail, or raised so that it can move without leaving a trail
- interfaces, cables and software to enable the computer running LOGO to control the turtle's movement

Systems tasks

OCR A OCR B

Evaluation of software components

Each user of software wants to be able to get the best results from that software. There are so many different types of software available that it is necessary to be very careful about choosing the best package for the purpose you have in mind. You need to consider:

> Exam questions sometimes ask you to evaluate software for use in a set context.

- what form **input** data will take
- what **processing** operations are required on this data
- what **output** is required

You then consider the characteristics of the various **packages** available, and how they fit your requirements.

KEY POINT

It is useful to develop a set of criteria to evaluate a software package.
a) Plan a framework for an evaluation report.
b) Scan read the software documentation to see whether:
  ● the program can be used to produce the outcome that you hope for;
  ● the package is easy to use.
c) Think of some suitable test data that can be used to run the program.
d) Make sure the program is user friendly.
e) Check that the methods of input and output suit what you want to do and the type of data you have.
f) If the program is interactive check the type of user interface suitable.
g) Find out if the program is versatile and adaptable.
h) Check the program is reliable.
i) Check the program is robust.
j) Check the program will validate all data before processing it.

PROGRESS CHECK

1. What is tailor made applications software?
2. What is general-purpose applications software?
3. What are applications packages?
4. Suggest what type of software package would be used for the following functions:
  ● to produce an interior design for a new aircraft
  ● to prepare a talk that will promote a new product
  ● to analyse data collected from a survey about people's holiday preferences
  ● to run a trial on projected use of a new bridge
5. What are the main questions you should ask yourself when choosing a software package?

1. Tailor made software, written specifically for a context, either in-house or by external experts.
2. General purpose packages, that provide typical software functions such as spreadsheets or databases and are non-specific.
3. Packages designed to perform a specific function or for use in a particular context.
4. CAD package; presentation package; spreadsheet package; modelling/simulation package.
5. What form any input data will take, what processing operations will be required on this data, and what kind of output would be most suitable. You should then look at the packages available, and see which best suits your criteria.

Sample GCSE questions

1. You have been asked to produce a school magazine. State what type of software you would use, and why.

   DTP package because it enables you to manipulate both images and text easily; it can colour separate. **[2]**

2. Environmental health authorities use a range of sensors to detect pollution.
   The results of their findings are presented as word-processed documents.
   One sensor is a water acidity detector. Describe four stages to show what happens to the data collected from the sensor.

   Example answer:

   One
   Data from sensors is stored in each sensor

   Two
   It is then transmitted to the computer

   Three
   Software is used to collect the data from the sensor and produce graphs of the results

   Four
   A word processor is used to present the test results **[4]**

   > *Try to answer this type of question in a logical order. Think about the main stages and try to use technical language.*

3. Most modern houses incorporate microprocessors in their central heating systems. Describe the role of the microprocessor in controlling the central heating and hot water system.

   Example answer:

   The microprocessor is linked to sensors on the hot water tank and thermostats located in the house, either fitted in rooms, or on each radiator. The system is also connected to a time clock. If the time clock tells the microprocessor that hot water or central heating is required, the processor checks to see if room temperature or hot water are below the settings on the thermostats. If necessary, it switches on the boiler and a water pump. It then controls a flow valve to direct hot water from the boiler either to radiators or to the hot water tank. **[6]**

   > *Try to list the types of device that the system would need, including sensors. For each device say what it would do.*

4. Complete each of the following sentences by stating a type of software that would be used in each instance.

   Minutes of a meeting would be typed using a

   word processing package.

Sample GCSE questions

Company accounts would be calculated using a

spreadsheet package.

The World Wide Web is accessed using a

web browser.

Customer details would be held on a

database.

Web pages are designed using

web design software.

Digital pictures can be manipulated using

image manipulation software. **[6]**

5. The office staff in a school use computers for word processing.

Give two examples of how text can be formatted using a word processor.

Example anwers:

Left/right justified; fully justified. **[2]**

> This type of question is easy to answer provided you think about text layout and use the correct terminology.

6. What software package would a shop manager use for the following:

Automatic calculation of daily sales

a spreadsheet

Production of advertising leaflets

desktop publishing software

A model of future potential sales

simulation/modelling software **[3]**

> Think about the data handling needs before you answer this type of question. Use generic software terms, e.g. spreadsheet software, not trade names, e.g. Excel.

7. The spreadsheet shown below is used to work out the pay for part time staff in a shop.

	A	B	C	D
1	Surname	Hours worked	Hourly rate	Pay
2	Markham	28	£4.30	
3	Singh	30	£4.60	
4	Rossellini	20	£4.90	
5	Jones	26	£4.60	
6	O'Mally	15	£4.30	
7	Oliver	20	£4.60	
8	TOTALS			

Sample GCSE questions

(a) Give the address of one cell that contains data about the type of currency used.

C2

[1]

Cells C3, C4, C5, C6 or C7 are also correct

(b) Cell D3 should automatically calculate the total salary of Mr Singh. Write down the formula that will be used in this cell.

*=B3*C3*

[2]

(c) Row 8 is used to summarise the total hours worked and total salaries. Write down the formula that will be inserted into cell B8 and the formula that will be inserted into cell D8.

=SUM(B2:B7), =SUM(D2:D7)

[4]

Use the =Sum( ) formula. Do not list each cell separately with + between each and don't forget the = sign.

8. A company designing kitchens uses Information Technology to:

● produce a catalogue of their products

● design the best arrangement for kitchen fitments

● calculate financial data

● control stock

Their computer system consists of computers, screens and keyboards.

(a) List three other pieces of equipment the company is likely to have to fulfil these requirements.

Scanner, mouse, printer.

[3]

(b) Alongside the use of a word processor, the company uses other software. Name one software package for each of the stated functions. For each piece of software, state what it would be used for.

Refer back to the lead on the question to help you decide what the company needs are.

1 *DTP software to produce catalogue;*

2 *3D design software (CAD) for kitchen layouts;*

3 *spreadsheet for finances;*

4 *database for stock control.*

[4]

Exam practice questions

> *The Learning Shop*
> *Watling Street West*
> *Towcester*
>
> 20ᵗʰ July 2001
>
> **Dear Member**
>
> *We thought you would like to know about some of the new activities that the centre is offering this winter. Alongside the ski trip planned for October there are a range of new activities.*
>
> The new activities include:
>
> | Activity | Level | Charge |
> |---|---|---|
> | Country walking | Beginners | £2.50 |
> | Rock climbing | Intermediate | £12.00 |
>
> We hope you will be able to take part in these activities.
>
> Yours sincerely
>
> Roger Knowles

---

1. (a) The font style used for the address is
   1. bold underlined ☐
   2. bold italic ☐
   3. regular ☐
   4. plain ☐   **[1]**

   (b) The date of the letter is
   1. fully justified ☐
   2. aligned right ☐
   3. aligned left ☐
   4. centred ☐   **[1]**

   (c) The main text of the letter is
   1. fully justified ☐
   2. aligned right ☐
   3. aligned left ☐
   4. centred ☐   **[1]**

Exam practice questions

(d) The lines describing the new activities are laid out using tabs. What type of tab has been used to align these items?
1. left ☐
2. right ☐
3. centre ☐
4. decimal ☐ **[1]**

(e) The text for the headings of the columns of new activities is
1. italic underlined ☐
2. bold ☐
3. lower case text ☐
4. regular text ☐ **[1]**

2. The following questions are based upon the spreadsheet shown below:

	A	B	C	D
1	**Surname**	**Hours worked**	**Hourly rate**	**Pay**
2	Markham	28	£ 4.30	120.40
3	Singh	30	£ 4.60	138.00
4	Rossellini	20	£ 4.90	98.00
5	Jones	26	£ 4.60	119.60
6	O'Mally	15	£ 4.30	64.50
7	Oliver	20	£ 4.60	92.00
8	TOTALS	139		

(a) Which row contains the spreadsheet column headings?
1. A ☐
2. 1 ☐
3. A11 ☐
4. A2 ☐ **[1]**

(b) The use of bold on the spreadsheet helps to
1. correct errors ☐
2. create a graph ☐
3. hide information ☐
4. emphasise the headings ☐ **[1]**

(c) The format of cells **C2** to **C7** is
1. date ☐
2. text ☐
3. currency ☐
4. percentage ☐ **[1]**

Exam practice questions

(d) The text in cell **A1** is
    1.   centred ☐
    2.   italic bold ☐
    3.   bold ☐
    4.   aligned right ☐ **[1]**

(e) The formula in cell **D2** to calculate total pay is
    1.   =(B2/E2) ☐
    2.   =B2*C2 ☐
    3.   =(B2+C2+D2) ☐
    4.   =AVERAGE(E2-F2) ☐ **[1]**

(f) When the correct formula is placed in **D2**, it can be replicated to cells
    1.   D3 to D7 ☐
    2.   D1 to D8 ☐
    3.   B2 to F2 ☐
    4.   E8 to F8 ☐ **[1]**

(g) The formula in cell **B8** to calculate the total hours worked is
    1.   =SUM(B1:E7) ☐
    2.   =SUM(F1:F8) ☐
    3.   =SUM(B2:B7) ☐
    4.   =SUM(F2:B8) ☐ **[1]**

(h) If the value in cell B6 is changed to 30, this automatically changes values displayed in cells
    1.   B8 and D6 ☐
    2.   A1 and D1 ☐
    3.   B8, B6 and D2 ☐
    4.   E7, B1 and B6 ☐ **[1]**

Exam practice questions

3. All the questions relate to a company database based upon the data shown below.

Human Resources Record		
Personal details		
Family name	**Given name**	**Gender**
Smith	Samantha	F
PAYE reference number	**Income tax code**	**National Insurance number**
3185	260L	YX 78 75 38 B
Job details		
Job title	**Job status**	**Hours worked**
Checker	Full time	37.5
Rate of pay	**Date employment started**	**Holiday entitlement**
£ 4.82/hour	15-02-02	25 days
Training record		
Induction training	**Health and safety training**	**Special skill training**
Yes	Yes	Not yet

(a) The data type of the Given name field is
   1. currency ☐
   2. number ☐
   3. date ☐
   4. text ☐ [1]

(b) The data type of the Rate of pay field is
   1. currency ☐
   2. number ☐
   3. date ☐
   4. text ☐ [1]

(c) In a database each column is a
   1. code ☐
   2. field ☐
   3. record ☐
   4. report ☐ [1]

Exam practice questions

(d) The database contains personal information; all personal information held by organisations should be
1. kept confidential ☐
2. held only as printed records ☐
3. checked for viruses ☐
4. corrected using a spell checker ☐ **[1]**

(e) To prevent unauthorised use of the database, access should be controlled by use of a
1. virus ☐
2. password ☐
3. CD-ROM ☐
4. directory ☐ **[1]**

(f) What would the company use to enter a photograph into a computer file so it can be used in the company newsletter?
1. a database ☐
2. a scanner ☐
3. a keyboard ☐
4. drawing tools ☐ **[1]**

(g) The most efficient way to send a letter to all employees on the database would be to use
1. manual data entry ☐
2. cut and paste ☐
3. mail-merge ☐
4. text entry ☐ **[1]**

4. Describe the three main types of user interface.

....
....
....
....
.... **[6]**

5. What are the typical functions of an operating system?

....
....
....
....
.... **[6]**

Exam practice questions

6. Describe the main types of programming languages, dividing them into low-level languages and high-level languages.

    ....

    ....

    ....

    ....

    .... **[4]**

7. What is machine code?

    ....

    ....

    ....

    ....

    .... **[4]**

8. Discuss criteria that you might use to evaluate a software package.

    ....

    ....

    ....

    ....

    .... **[3]**

The following topics are covered in this chapter:

- 4.1 Networks and communications
- 4.2 Computer to computer communication
- 4.3 External communications links
- 4.4 What is the Internet?
- 4.5 Email
- 4.6 Entering data

4.1 Networks and communications

LEARNING SUMMARY

After completing this section you should be able to:

- understand that information systems can be linked together on a world-wide scale
- explain the terms real-time processing, and batch processing

An information system allows communication between a **human user**, the **devices** that make up the hardware of the system, and the software that performs **systems functions** and user applications. **Data** is entered into the system and information is gained as **output**.

Communication also takes place on a much wider scale.

KEY POINT

Telecommunications and networks link computers of all kinds all over the world. It is becoming more and more common for people to work from a home base, electronically linked to world-wide communications systems.

Remember ICT refers to more than just computers. Fax machines, TV, the Internet and mobile phones are all part of ICT.

Exam questions sometimes ask you to describe how ICT has led to more people working from home. Try to use the correct terms.

You may be required to describe a computer system in use.

Some people use the word **'telecommute'** to describe working at a job from a home office with the aid of a computer, **Internet link**, **telephone**, **fax** and other specialised electronic equipment.

A travel agency provides a good example of the use of telecommunications with computers to provide customer services. The agency uses an on-line enquiry and booking system where a terminal in the agency office is connected to the main processor via a telecommunications link. The terminal can be either a **dumb terminal**, which is simply a screen and a keyboard, or a **smart terminal**, which is a screen, keyboard and processor with some backing store. The telecommunications link can be a telephone line, microwave link or radio link.

The system is likely to be interactive. This means that when a travel agency employee wants to access the system, he or she will start by entering data (perhaps the agency's official reference number) on an opening screen. Each time the employee enters an item or items of data on a particular screen, the system will reply with further screens and prompts for more data until an outcome is obtained.

In effect, the computer system has a conversation with the travel agency employee in order to achieve a particular task such as booking an airline ticket for a passenger. Many airline and other travel tickets are now electronic. No printed ticket is issued at all. For example, the traveller is told when to travel by information produced at the time of booking, arrives at the airport and goes to the appropriate check-in desk, where all of the necessary information is available on the computer terminal to allow the passenger to travel.

Real-time processing

OCR A
EDEXCEL
AQA A   AQA B
WJEC

Real-time processing is also used in the context of many retail stores, and in warehouses. As soon as an item is sold or used, the system immediately deducts it from stock, so that the stock position is always accurate.

Airlines and many other booking systems use **real-time processing** for **transactions** like the process described above.

Whenever a transaction occurs, the system is **automatically updated**, whatever the time is. In the case of airline booking, this avoids double-booking of seats. Where one traveller books a ticket at one travel agency, and it is the last available seat on the plane, **real-time processing** immediately allows the system to note that the plane is now full, so that, if another passenger tries to book a ticket on the same plane a few minutes later, the **display** will show that there are no more seats.

KEY POINT
Real-time processing is essential in control systems, where data from sensors is entered into the system and processed to provide immediate feedback to the device being controlled. It would be a traffic disaster if traffic lights changed 20 minutes after sensors registered a large number of vehicles waiting. Similarly, if a robot did not carry out its task at exactly the right moment on a production line, there could be chaos.

Batch processing

OCR A
EDEXCEL
AQA A   AQA B
WJEC

Batch processing is used in contexts where it makes sense to collect together a lot of inputs of different kinds and then process them all in one go, or batch. A gas supply company, for example, is likely to use batch processing to produce its bills. Data of several different kinds will be processed in the batch to produce the bills. This will include customers' account numbers, previous gas meter readings, present gas meter readings, any new customers and different tariffs (gas supply prices) that may be offered.

KEY POINT
The advantage of batch processing is that the computer operator can enter all the data for one batch in one operation. The software will carry out the various processes required and the final result is a bill for each customer, and an updated master file of customer information.

PROGRESS CHECK

1. What is the difference between a dumb terminal and a smart terminal?
2. Explain what is meant by real-time processing.
3. Explain what is meant by batch processing.
4. What is a telecommuter?

1. A dumb terminal is simply a screen and keyboard forming part of a network and linked to a main processor via a telecommunications link. A smart terminal forms part of a network in the same way, but includes a processor with some backing store.
2. Any data entered into an information system is processed immediately, regardless of the time of day. This is important in a booking system, for example, to avoid double bookings.
3. Data is entered into the system, but is not processed until an operator gives the command to process the whole batch.
4. Someone who works from a home office, but, by using telecommunications links, enjoys the benefits of worldwide connections via the Internet.

4.2 Computer to computer communication

After completing this section you should be able to:

LEARNING SUMMARY

- explain what is meant by a network
- define a Local Area Network and discuss its advantages and disadvantages
- define a Wide Area Network and discuss its advantages and disadvantages
- describe the software and devices that make up a network, including cables, connectors and network cards, and typical hardware devices
- explain the features of the four main ways of laying out a network: ring, line, star and hierarchical

You should know the benefits of networking computers and the main types of networks.

Exam questions often ask for the difference between LANs and WANs.

Communication between two or more computer systems is achieved by setting up a **network**. The computer systems are linked so that they can **'talk'** to each other, share **computing power** and/or **storage facilities**.

The link may be between computers in one building, or it could be between computers in different parts of the world. The term **network** includes the individual computer systems, the **connections** and the **hardware** that allows communication to happen.

A network may include a **dedicated file server**. This is normally one computer in the network that has a much higher **specification** than the others, with a very large hard disk drive. All data common to the network will be held on the dedicated server. It will also monitor and control the network and while it is performing this very important task, it will not be available for use as an interactive work station.

KEY POINT

Networks are divided into two types, LANs (Local Area Networks) and WANs (Wide Area Networks).

LANs – Local Area Networks

OCR A **OCR B**
EDEXCEL

A LAN is confined to a small area, usually within a single building.

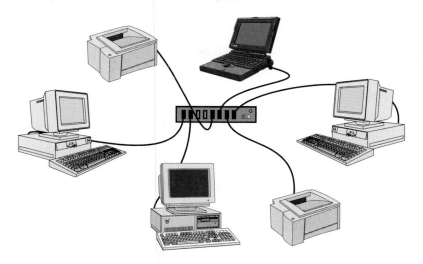

LAN

> You must be able to describe a system in terms of advantages and disadvantages. Do not always remember the good points.

> A line (bus) topology is the cheapest in terms of cabling costs.

> The setting up of hierarchical system passwords to allow different users different access is the key to controlling access to most company databases.

Advantages of LANs:

- Costly resources such as printers can be shared by all of the computers. This means that better quality printing is available to everyone because one or two expensive, high specification printers can be bought instead of several cheaper, lower specification models.

- Central backing store can be provided in one place (the dedicated file server) so all work is saved together. An individual user can load his or her work on any computer on the network.

- Software can be shared, and upgrading is easier too. This gives continuity in the workplace. However, sharing software is often not much cheaper than providing a copy for each machine because a licence has to be bought for each copy of the software needed.

- Central back-up can take place automatically at regular intervals. A user will usually be able to retrieve work that has been deleted by mistake.

- Data can be shared across the network. For example, this would allow several people to work on the same project.

- If the data being shared is in a database, several people will be able to use the database at the same time, but they will not be able to edit the same record at the same time. When a record is opened by one user, it is locked so that other people cannot try to edit it at the same time. This avoids the confusion that would result if several people were trying to edit data at the same time. Once the first user has completed and saved the operation, the record is unlocked again.

- Local email messages can be sent to people working at other terminals on the network. This can save time and ensures that messages get to the right place.

- There may be a local **Intranet**. This works like the World Wide Web, with pages of information. The difference is that the pages can be accessed only over the LAN. As it does not involve phone links, an Intranet is free.

Disadvantages of LANs:

Rings provide the fastest form of local area networking.

- The use of email within the **network** can lead to problems of time wasting as people send messages that do not relate to work. Some companies discourage the use of in-house email because they believe that it is better for employees to communicate face to face.

- Where a lot of **terminals** are served by only one or two printers, long print queues may develop, causing people to have to wait for printed output.

- **Network security** can be a problem. If a virus gets into one computer, it is likely to spread quickly across the network because it will get into the central backing store.

Try to remember at least three advantages and three disadvantages for each system. Look carefully at the exam question to see how many points the examiner wants.

- Users of the network have to have **user names** and **passwords**. Some users are not very good at keeping passwords secret, or they may use passwords that are easy to guess. Other people can then log onto the network.

- If the **dedicated file server** fails, work stored on shared hard disk drives will not be accessible and it will not be possible to use network printers either.

- Cabling can be expensive to buy and to install. In a busy office situation, cabling must often be placed under the floor so that people will not trip over it. If connecting cables are damaged, some sections of the **network** can become isolated. They will not be able to communicate with the rest of the network.

WANs – Wide Area Networks

OCR A   OCR B
EDEXCEL
AQA A   AQA B
WJEC

A **Wide Area Network** is not confined to one building. The computers and **terminals** forming part of the network can be spread around the world.

External communication links such as **satellites**, **microwaves** or **telecommunication links** will be used to connect the network. The connection must normally be paid for because the links are external.

The Internet is really a vast Wide Area Network.

LANs may be connected to WANs via a special gateway. Many Local Area Networks will be connected to the Internet in this way.

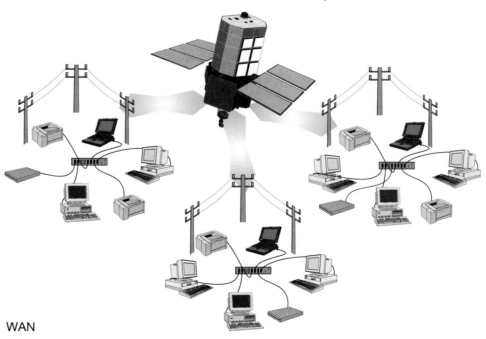

WAN

> **KEY POINT**
>
> **Advantages/Disadvantages of WANs**
>
> Advantages and disadvantages of using Wide Area Networks are very similar to those for Local Area Networks, but on a larger scale. Security is even more important, particularly where WANs are connected to the public telephone system.

Formation of a network – components

EDEXCEL

A **network** is not just a number of computers connected by **cables**. Parts found in a typical network are:

Network software

This may be part of the **operating system**, or it can be software designed specifically to manage a network.

Cables

Connecting cables are usually used to **connect devices** on a network, although some networks make use of **radio** or **microwaves** to provide the link. Cables vary in both performance and cost.

Connectors

Connectors are used to connect **network cables** to **terminals** or other devices.

> You will not be expected to be specific about any particular network hardware and software but you should know what each component does.

Network cards

If a personal computer is to be used as a **terminal** in a **network**, a device called a **network card** must be built into it.

The network card looks like a small **circuit board** and slots into one of the connectors on the main circuit board (called the **mother board**) inside the computer.

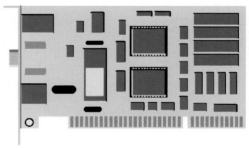

Network card

Network cards have **connectors** on them for **network cables**. The planning of the communication links between each of these devices (called **nodes**) must be carried out carefully. There are a number of different ways in which nodes are commonly linked. These ways are called **topologies**, and there are four common network topologies, called **ring**, **line** (**bus**), **star** and **hierarchical**.

> You will be expected to know about the ways a network can be constructed. You should be able to draw a simple line diagram to represent each.

> Think about the advantages of using a network in terms of hardware sharing and data sharing.

> **KEY POINT**
>
> Typical hardware devices that may form part of a network are:
> - personal computers used as terminals
> - one or more central processing units acting as dedicated file servers or print servers
> - disk drives
> - scanners
> - printers
> - point-of-sale terminals (in a retail setting)

Ring topology

OCR A OCR B
EDEXCEL
AQA A AQA B
WJEC

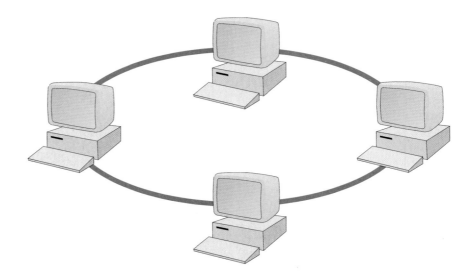

> **Although the computers are connected in a circle they do not need to be placed in one.**

In a **ring topology**, all of the terminals or other nodes in the network are connected together in a circle, with no **device** having any more importance than any other.

> **KEY POINT**
>
> An obvious disadvantage is that if there is a fault in any part of the circle, all of the nodes will be affected.

Line (bus) topology

OCR A OCR B
EDEXCEL
AQA A AQA B
WJEC

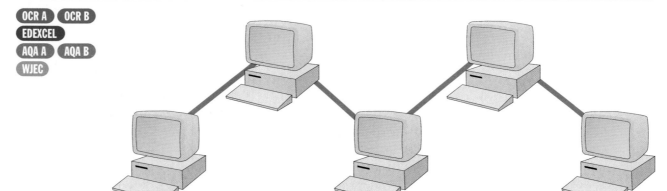

In this system, data is sent to all **nodes** on the network at the same time. **Devices** are positioned along a line, rather like bus stops.

> **KEY POINT**
>
> As in the ring topology, each device has equal status, but the advantage here is that, if one terminal is not working correctly, the others are not affected. This type of network is cheap and reliable.

Star topology

OCR A   OCR B
EDEXCEL
AQA A   AQA B
WJEC

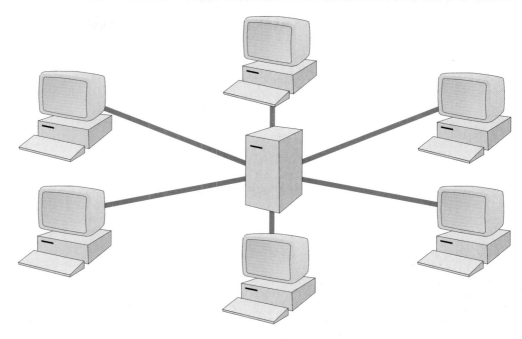

In this type of **network**, a **central controller** forms the **principal node**, while the subsidiary nodes form the points of the star.

> **KEY POINT**
>
> As the central machine controls the whole system, the whole system will be affected if it breaks down. Star topologies use more cabling than other topologies and this makes them more expensive. However, communication is fast because there is a direct path from the central controller to each terminal.

Hierarchical network

OCR A   OCR B
EDEXCEL
AQA A   AQA B
WJEC

In a **hierarchical network**, one or more computers is more powerful than the rest. The relationship between the nodes is called a **client–server relationship**. The more powerful **server**, (or servers), looks after **printing**, **file maintenance** and other **peripherals**.

> **KEY POINT**
>
> Less powerful computers called clients are connected to the network. The clients may have no disk drives nor processing power of their own. They make use of the functions provided by the server.

Where a file server is a dedicated file server, it cannot be used as a terminal and will be occupied all the time in managing the network.

There are two types of server, the **file server** and the **print server**.

The **file server** is used to store both programs and data. It acts as a massive **hard drive** on behalf of all the **client terminals**.

The print server

The print server is a computer in the **network** that has a printer attached. It manages all print requests from client terminals.

> **KEY POINT**
>
> **The advantage is that the client terminals are not tied up managing their own printers, but, as mentioned in network disadvantages (page 86), long print queues can build up sometimes.**

PROGRESS CHECK

1. What is a network?
2. Explain what a Wide Area Network is.
3. State one advantage and one disadvantage of a WAN.
4. Describe the software that makes up a network.
5. Describe the software and devices that make up a network.

1. An arrangement of two or more computers that are linked electronically so that they can communicate, share processing power and/or storage facilities. A network may include a dedicated file server, but does not have to.
2. A Wide Area Network is not confined to one building. The hardware that forms part of the network can be spread around the world.
3. Advantages and disadvantages of WANs are the same as for LANs, but on a larger scale. WANs can share information around the world. The connection must normally be paid for because the links are external. Security is of particular importance.
4. A network is controlled by network software. This may be part of the operating system, or it can be designed specifically to manage the network.
5. Cables and connectors are required to link hardware devices together, and network cards are built into computers used as terminals in a network. Other typical hardware devices that may form part of a standard network are: One or more central processing units acting as dedicated file servers or print servers, disk drives, scanners and printers.

4.3 External communications links

LEARNING SUMMARY

After completing this section you should be able to:

● **describe the function of a modem**
● **understand the importance of data transmission rate**
● **explain what is meant by ISDN**
● **list the advantages of ISDN over modems**
● **explain the significance of bandwidth**

Modems

OCR A   OCR B
WJEC

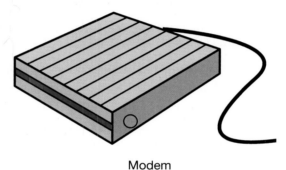

Modem

> You will be expected to know the differences including advantages and disadvantages of modems and ISDN.

A modem is a device that connects a computer to a **telephone line**, or other **external communication link** such as television cables (**coaxial cables** or **fibre optics**), or **microwaves**.

The name modem is short for **mo**dulator–**dem**odulator and its function is to **encode data** so that it can be transmitted, both from and to the computer.

> **KEY POINT**
>
> The digital signals from one computer are converted by the modem into analogue signals for transmission, and when they reach the modem at the destination computer, the signals are converted back into digital form.

> You should understand how faster modems have a higher baud rate.

Important features of modems are:

● Data transmission rate. The speed at which data is transferred is very important. This is because the user is connected to a telephone line, and the use of this line costs money.

● Users also do not want to sit in front of a screen and have to wait ages for files to be **downloaded**.

> Do not confuse bit rate with baud rate.

● Speed is either measured in **baud** (a unit that measures the speed with which data is transferred) or in **bits per second**.

> **KEY POINT**
> Some modems are able to compress data before sending it, which reduces transmission time and cost.

When a connection is made, the modem at each end negotiates with the other modem – they check each other's capabilities and settle on a suitable data transmission rate, and procedure for correcting any errors (see bandwidth page 93).

> **KEY POINT**
> - **Automatic dialling.** Almost all modems now perform automatic dialling and can accept other communications commands from the computer.
> - **Fax compatibility.** Some modems are compatible with fax machines and, with suitable software, can send and receive fax messages.
> - **Internal or external location.** An internal modem fits inside the computer. An external modem connects to the computer by means of a cable to the computer's serial port (see below).

Digital networks

Telephone line modems are gradually being replaced by digital network cables that connect direct to users' businesses and homes. These are known as **cable modems**.

> **KEY POINT**
> Modems can be connected to the serial, parallel or USB ports.

The parallel interface on the back of a computer is sometimes called the printer interface.

The **serial port** is a connection that allows a computer to transmit data to another device using **serial transmission**. This means one bit at a time. It is common for a computer to be connected to a printer or modem via a serial port.

You should understand the differences between parallel and serial ports and how they are used.

A **parallel port** is a connection that allows the computer to transmit data using **parallel transmission**, where several bits are sent simultaneously over separate wires. A parallel port may be connected to a printer, in which case the printer will be known as a **parallel printer**.

Modern computers also often have a **Universal Serial Port** (**USB**). Devices can be connected to this port without switching the computer off first.

ISDN

ISDN – **Integrated Services Digital Network** – is a service provided by telecommunications companies such as British Telecom to enable ordinary telephone lines to carry **digital signals**. This means that a modem is not needed to convert signals into **analogue form**. Instead, a device called an **ISDN terminal adapter** is required. It uses a technique whereby several digital signals can be sent along the same wire. This means that the user can use the telephone, and send or receive data at the same time.

KEY POINT

Advantages of ISDN compared with modems:

● The use of ISDN means that data can be transmitted much faster than when a modem is used.

● Data can also be compressed before sending, which increases transmission speed still further.

● Because ISDN equipment is relatively inexpensive, it makes video conferencing accessible to many people. Through a network, typically the Internet, they can talk to and see other people in distant places, and send and receive data at the same time.

Bandwidth

OCR A   OCR B
EDEXCEL
AQA A   AQA B

This term is used to describe the **transmission capacity** of the medium that is transmitting data across a network. Telephone cables, for example, have a lower **bandwidth** than **fibre optic cables**.

They can transmit a lower range of frequencies.

High bandwidth allows transmission of many signals at once. On a monitor screen, high bandwidth provides a sharp image.

PROGRESS CHECK

1. What is the function of a modem?
2. Explain why the rate of data transmission is important.
3. Explain the term ISDN.
4. Give brief details of any advantages of using ISDN rather than a modem.
5. Why is bandwidth important?

5. It refers to the speed at which data can be transferred across a network. High bandwidth is preferable because it allows transmission of many signals at once. On a monitor screen, high bandwidth provides a sharp image.

4. Using ISDN, data can be transmitted much faster than when a modem is used. Data can also be compressed before sending, which increases transmission speed still further. Because ISDN equipment is not too expensive, it makes video conferencing accessible to many people. They can talk to and see other people in distant places, and send and receive data at the same time.

3. Integrated Services Digital Network is a service provided by companies such as British Telecom to enable ordinary telephone lines to carry digital signals. A device called an ISDN terminal adapter is required. It allows several digital signals to be sent along the same wire so that the user can make a phone call, and send or receive data at the same time.

2. Because the user is connected to a telephone line, and the use of this line costs money. Users also do not want to sit in front of a screen and have to wait ages for files to be downloaded.

1. It connects a computer to a telephone line, or other external communication link such as television cables or microwaves. Its function is to encode data so that it can be transmitted, both from and to the computer.

4.4 What is the Internet?

LEARNING SUMMARY

After completing this section you should be able to:

- *give a brief description of what the Internet is, and explain the term World Wide Web*
- *list the requirements for a connection to the Internet*
- *list typical customer services provided by an Internet Service Provider*
- *explain the meaning of the term protocols in relation to the Internet*
- *describe how the World Wide Web is used*
- *explain what a web site is*
- *explain in detail how to use a search engine to locate information*

When people talk about the Internet, they often mean the World Wide Web. This is the fastest growing part of the Internet and it takes the form of pages where graphics, sound, video and animation are used with text to present information on every topic.

The Internet is really a **world-wide** area network of **wide area networks** – the biggest network in the world. Some of the computers on the Internet are small PCs, while others are huge **supercomputers**. Because the data held on any of these computers can be accessed by any other computer, the Internet can offer a vast amount of information. Data can also be passed around the world very rapidly.

KEY POINT

The pages on the World Wide Web are organised into sites and the mix of media used in a site is called hypertext. Hypertext links are built into the World Wide Web, and these allow the user to move around by clicking on words or graphics on the screen. The user interface that is thus provided by the World Wide Web is both attractive and easy to use.

Requirements for connection to Internet

OCR A   OCR B
EDEXCEL
AQA A   AQA B
NICCEA

The development of the Internet has given rise to a large amount of jargon – language specially created for the purpose. Try to remember the key terms and what they stand for.

You may need to describe how to connect to the web as part of an examination question.

A user can have either a permanent Internet connection, or a temporary one. Some business organisations or universities have permanent connections, but it is more common to have a temporary connection. It is common to use a modem to provide the link from a personal computer to a service called an Internet Service Provider (ISP), which offers a permanent link, or node, into the Internet. The user's modem will dial the ISP, which maintains what is called a point of presence (PoP) – rather like a reception area. The ISP will check that the user's password is valid before allowing access to its file server, and it will normally offer a range of 'customer services' as well as access to the Internet.

The 'customer services' may include:

- access to news, weather, sport, financial pages
- message boards – users can have discussions, or post a message and wait for replies
- electronic mail – anyone connected to the Internet can be contacted
- instant messages – users can hold conversations
- directories of members, giving details of similar interests
- offers of free software and demonstrations
- member services – keeping track of on-line costs
- access to on-line shopping – many on-line stores provide goods at very attractive prices

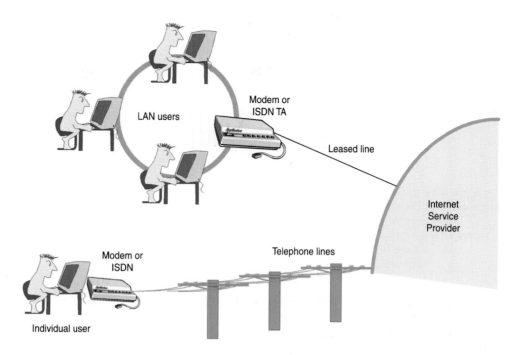

It is usually wise for a user to choose an **ISP** located near by. In addition to paying some sort of **subscription** to the ISP, the user will often have to pay the cost of telephone charges once his or her modem has provided a connection. (Once the connection is made, the user is said to be **on line**.)

Local rate telephone calls are cheaper than long distance calls.

The cost of accessing the Internet is being reduced as ISPs and telecommunications companies offer a range of special deals to the millions of people who wish to use the Internet. When setting up an Internet connection, it is always worth shopping around to see who is offering the best deals. Some providers offer free connection and an allocation of free calls. Others offer unlimited calls for a set annual or monthly fee.

> **KEY POINT**
>
> The modem is said to be dialling-up when it connects to the Internet. In the same way, files sent to the Internet are up-loaded, while files taken from the Internet are down-loaded. Because of costs involved, the data transmission speed of a modem is particularly important when accessing the Internet.

Software

OCR A OCR B
EDEXCEL
AQA A AQA B
NICCEA

Software is also needed to make a connection to the Internet. Standards, or **protocols**, have been developed in order to improve speed and reliability of **data transfer** over the Internet.

> **KEY POINT**
>
> - **TCP/IP** (Transmission Control Protocol/Internet Protocol) **system software needs to be running on the computer.**
> - **The function of the** TCP **part of the package is to break data up into manageable** chunks **or** packets **that bear the address they are being sent to.**
> - **The** IP **part of the package routes the packets from machine to machine, and the** TCP **part then puts data back together in the correct order so that it can be used.**

Do not forget to include software and hardware if you are asked to describe how to connect to the Internet.

These **functions** are very important because of the way the Internet works. If you are sending a message from the United Kingdom to the United States, for example, the **first packet of data** may be sent via France and Sweden, while the **second packet** could travel via a satellite link to Australia and on.

> **KEY POINT**
> The route does not matter as TCP/IP will make sure that the packets arrive in the correct place and are reassembled in the correct order, even if the first packet arrives last.

If you wish to allow other users on the web to access your computer you must have a fixed IP address.

The **protocol** requires that every computer linked to the **TCP/IP** network should have a **unique IP (Internet Protocol) address**. The address can be just numeric, composed of four numbers, each between 0 and 255, separated by dots. An example would be:

195.107.24.242.

These numbers are given out by **Internet Service Providers** to ensure that the same number is not given out twice. Its unique number means that any computer on the Internet can be recognised, no matter where it is located. An **IP** number can have a name attached to it to give the address more meaning.

A further piece of software is needed wherever the connection to the Internet is made through a **modem** and **ISP**. The software will enable the modem to dial-up the telephone number to reach the service provider, and will allow **TCP/IP** to operate on the computer.

Common Internet services and their features

The Internet offers a vast range of services and one of the most significant of these is the World Wide Web.

Use of the World Wide Web

Specialised software called a **web browser** is needed to make use of the features of the **World Wide Web** (**WWW**). The different packages on offer work in similar ways.

Sometimes exam questions ask you to describe the uses of the Web.

The **WWW** is divided into millions of sites called **websites**. These are **files** made of **groups of pages**, designed and set up by companies or individuals who wish to communicate with Internet users throughout the world.

The aim may be simply to **spread information**, talk to other people, or to sell, or find, services or products.

> **KEY POINT**
> - Each website has its own unique address, **which is called the Uniform Resource Locator (URL). If you know the URL of the site you are looking for, you can type this straight into the address prompt of the browser.**
> - **The address will take a standard format, and the full form of the address will start http://www......... http stands for** Hypertext Transfer Protocol, **the standard method of publishing information as hypertext (see above) on the Internet. Many browsers will accept a URL without the http:// part of it.**

You will not be expected to know the language HTML but you will be expected to know what HTML means and why it is important.

Web pages are written in a programming language called **Hyper Text Markup Language** (**HTML**) and the web browser automatically recognises these pages and tries to display them.

Home pages

OCR A   OCR B
EDEXCEL
AQA A   AQA B
WJEC

The home page is normally the first thing that you see when you first access a **site**. The home page provides an introduction to the site, with **hypertext links** (see above) to all the other pages of the site, and possibly to other sites also.

> **KEY POINT**
> The home page **is designed to help users to move around the site.** Links **can be recognised easily on a page. In text, they are usually a different colour from the rest of the text, and they are often underlined. Pictures and icons can also be links and these can be spotted by moving the cursor over them. The cursor is normally an arrow, but it changes to a hand with a pointing finger when it moves over a link.**

If a user wants to visit certain sites on a regular basis, the **browser** can **bookmark** the **URLs** of these sites so that they can be accessed quickly without having to type in the address. A user can start on any **WWW** page in any site and follow **links** leading to other pages in other sites. This type of exploration, or browsing, of the World Wide Web is called **surfing**.

Using a search engine

OCR A   OCR B
EDEXCEL
AQA A   AQA B
WJEC
Key Skills

Surfing may be entertaining, but a user often needs to locate specific information relating to a particular topic. Software called a **search engine** is used in this case. A search engine is a program that is able to search through large quantities of text and other **data**, according to specific instructions that it has been given.

KEY POINT

> There will usually be a choice of search engines that can be accessed through the search button on the toolbar. Given the same starting information, each of these may produce different results because they search in different ways. A search engine will normally request key words to describe what a user is looking for and there are several ways of searching:
> - If you type in the key words *traffic jams*, a search engine will search for all documents that contain *traffic* and/or *jams*, giving highest priority to those that contain both words. This could result in a long and confusing list of possible contacts.
> - If only lower case letters are used, the search will find documents that contain the words regardless of whether they are in lower or upper case. If a mixture of upper and lower case is specified, the search will try to find words that match the words exactly – *Traffic jams*.
> - You can place double quotation marks around the phrase to make sure that the search engine finds only the documents where the words appear in that order.

> Learning how to structure a search is very important. Exam questions sometimes ask you to construct a set of search criteria.

Search criteria are used to reduce the size of the list of contacts produced, but it will still often be necessary to use more precise search instructions (carry out an advanced search):

Advanced searches

OCR A   OCR B
EDEXCEL
AQA A   AQA B
WJEC
Key Skills

Search engines have slightly different requirements for carrying out advanced searches. The general rules are as follows:

+ and −

- If you put a + in front of a word, documents will be found that contain that word. +traffic+jams will find all documents that contain the word traffic and also the word jams.

- traffic+jams would give a list of documents that contain the word jams but will not necessarily be about traffic.

- If you put a − in front of a word, documents will be found that do not contain that word.

- +traffic−jams would give a list of documents that contain the word traffic but miss out those that contain jams.

AND, OR, AND NOT

The word **AND** can be used to combine key words. All words joined by AND must be contained in the document for it to be listed in the results of a search.

OR can be used to combine key words. At least one of the words joined by OR must be contained in the document for it to be listed in the results of the search. OR is often used to link words that have a similar meaning in a search, for example jam OR marmalade.

AND NOT is also used to combine key words. The search will not include documents containing the word following AND NOT. For example jam AND NOT marmalade would produce documents relating to jam, but not any containing the word marmalade.

> You must learn how to use AND, OR and NOT as part of your search criteria.

Brackets

Brackets are used in searches in the same way as they are used in mathematics. They can group words together to make a more complex search possible. For example,

horses AND (dogs OR cats)

would produce a list of documents containing the word horses and either the word dogs, or cats, or both.

Wild card

The character * is called a wild card and can be used to stand for any character or set of characters. For example, typing auto* would produce a list of documents containing words such as automobile, automatic, autogiro, autopsy, and so on.

Titles

Rather than searching whole documents or web sites for key words, a search can be limited to the titles of documents or websites. If the words are important to the document or web site, they may well be contained in the title. The search engine is instructed to do this by typing t: before the key word(s). For example,

t: "fuel shortage" would search titles containing those words, in that order.

PROGRESS CHECK

1. Outline briefly what the Internet is.
2. What does the term World Wide Web refer to?
3. What devices and/or software does a user need to connect to the Internet?
4. List briefly the customer services typically offered by an Internet Service Provider.
5. What is a web site?

1. The Internet is a world-wide network of wide area networks – the biggest network in the world.
2. The World Wide Web is the fastest growing part of the Internet and it takes the form of web sites organised into pages where graphics, sound, video and animation are used with text to present information on every topic.
3. The user must set up an account with an Internet Service Provider, who provides the link to the Internet. A modem is needed to connect to the ISP. Internet standard software is needed (TCP/IP) to allow data transmission, also specialised software to enable the modem to dial-up to the ISP.
4. The ISP provides a customer with a link to the Internet. It can also offer access to news, weather, sport and financial pages; message boards; an email service; instant messages; members' directories; free software and software demonstrations; account services for members and access to on-line shopping.
5. A file made of groups of pages that can be displayed on the World Wide Web. Each web site has its own unique address, which is called the Uniform Resource Locator (URL).

4.5 Email

Email is another important facility offered by the Internet, and its use is increasing every day.

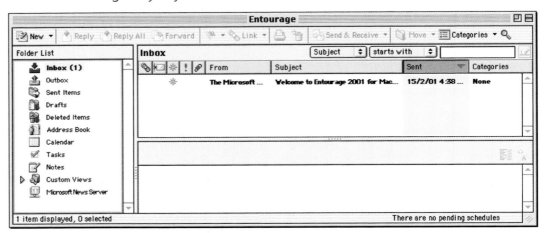

It is a method of sending messages from one **terminal** to another via a communications link.

As with all other **computer functions**, it requires the appropriate software. You also need to have an email account, which is usually supplied by the Internet Service Provider that you use. You can then have an **email address**, which must be different from anyone else's address. To send a message, you also need to know the email address of the person you are sending it to.

Exam questions often ask you to describe how to send an email.

The **software** provides the **interface** for writing and addressing the message. It also displays **messages received**, and provides functions such as an **address book** and **diary**.

Messages can be written, and any documents **attached** to them, while the computer is **off-line**. This helps to keep costs down. Telephone charges are only incurred while actually sending and receiving messages.

KEY POINT

● When the message is finished, it can be sent to an Outbox in the source computer. The same message can be sent to many different people, simply by adding their email addresses to the address box.
● You will then use your communications software and modem to connect to the ISP's file server. Once connected, you can tell the system to transmit the message, and to receive any incoming messages, which will go into an Inbox.
● The sent message is placed in a mail box on a main computer.
● As soon as the person to whom you have sent the message logs on (connects his or her computer system to the Internet), he or she can access their mail box and, when the incoming message has been transmitted to the Inbox, read the message.

Email and the World Wide Web

EDEXCEL

WJEC

Advantages:

- Email provides a quick way of sending messages all around the world.
- People often feel that it is all right to send a quick message by email whereas, with a traditional letter or telephone call, they have to spend more time.
- The email can be printed, so it can be kept like a traditional letter and, in a commercial context, could provide valuable proof that a person has agreed to something.
- The same message can be sent to many recipients at the same time.
- Documents prepared in many types of software can be attached to emails and sent with them. This includes pictures and video clips.
- Users of email can join mailing lists covering specific topics. These give interested people a chance to get together and talk about a subject by email. Regular updates can be sent out on particular issues.
- The World Wide Web provides an almost limitless source of information and, if it is used carefully, can provide valuable information for research of all kinds.
- The results of research can be published immediately on the Web so that information available is always up-to-date.

> **Exam questions often ask for the advantages and disadvantages of email over traditional mail.**

Disadvantages:

- In working situations, the use of email, and surfing the World Wide Web, can lead to a lot of time wasting.
- Messages deliberately designed to cause trouble, or upset people, can easily be sent to many targets.
- Young people may gain access to sites that are not designed for them and may contain unsuitable material.
- Some people would say that certain users, often young people, become 'addicted' to surfing the Web and are no longer interested in other activities.
- Viruses can easily be sent to millions of recipients and can cause massive system breakdowns.
- A lot of 'junk mail' can be sent. In addition to being unwanted, the recipient has to pay telephone charges while this mail is downloaded.
- The Internet is widely used as a source of up-to-date reference material, but there is no way of checking the quality of information displayed on web pages. It is quite possible for unscrupulous operators to display information that is quite untrue (see checking data below). Try to remember at least four advantages and four disadvantages.

PROGRESS CHECK

1. What is electronic mail (email)?
2. What is the simplest way of minimising costs when sending emails?
3. When you press 'Send' after writing a message, will it automatically be sent?

1. An important facility offered by the Internet. It is a method of sending messages from one terminal to another via a communications link, allowing people all over the world to contact each other quickly and inexpensively.
2. Costs are minimised by preparing messages with the system off-line. This means actually writing the message and attaching any documents before logging on.
3. You must log on first, but you must also use your communications software and modem to connect to the ISP's file server in order to tell the system to transmit the message. This is normally done by pressing 'Send and Receive'.

4.6 Entering data

After completing this section you should be able to:

● explain why data may be entered into an information system in code form
● list points to remember when designing codes
● explain the structures for organising data that is stored in an information system

Encoding data/information

EDEXCEL

Data is often entered into an **information system** in code form. There may be a number of reasons for this, such as:

● codes can be typed in more quickly, and make subsequent searches faster too
● using codes reduces the size of **files**, so that **data processing** is faster
● codes are often **unique**. For example, each product in a supermarket will have a **unique code**. If a search were carried out without a code, and a more general term such as 'corn flakes' were keyed in to start the search, it would locate more items than keying in the code that would find the specific type of corn flakes required

> **You will not be expected to remember codes but should know where they are used.**

> **KEY POINT**
>
> There are certain important points to remember when designing codes:
> ● They must be easy to use. If operators find codes impossible to remember, or long and awkward, they will not want to use them.
> ● Codes should always be the same length. This then provides an easy way of performing a validation check on them (see checking data on input section). If the code is too long or too short, it is obvious that a mistake has been made.
> ● Codes must not be too short. Although short codes are easier to enter, there is more likelihood of running out of codes, and, where security is an important issue, short codes are easier to break and copy.

Data/information structures and storage of data

AQA A   **AQA B**

> **You will be expected to understand the terms files, data, fields and records. You should also understand why each is important.**

> **The term *field* also refers to a place where information is entered on a screen. For example, a cell in a spreadsheet where a product price is to be entered is a field.**

Huge quantities of data are entered into the average information system. It is vital that the data stored in that system is organised in a methodical way so that it is accessible. All data is stored in **files**, which have to have **file names**.

Within each file, data is divided into **records**. A record may contain just one piece of data. In this case it is said to have a single **field**. It may, on the other hand, contain many pieces of related data items, in many fields. For example, a company may store information about each employee in a single record. Each record will consist of a number of fields, one for the name of the employee, one for the National Insurance number, one for the street address, and so on.

A **field** holds just one piece of data. For example, in an address list, the postcode part of the address might be stored in one field containing the right number of characters for the postcode.

Key field

OCR A   OCR B
EDEXCEL
AQA A   AQA B
WJEC

> A key field must be unique. No two people can have the same reference.

This is a term used to describe a **field** that is unique to a particular record and that can therefore be used to search a file to locate the record quickly. For example, each employee in a large company may be given a unique employee number. Using the number as the key field, the employee's record can easily be found in the company's information system.

Text files – numbers and/or letters

OCR A   OCR B
EDEXCEL
AQA A   AQA B
WJEC

> You will not be expected to remember different types of files, for example .doc used by Microsoft Word. You should understand that different types of software save files with different file extensions.

A text file is a file that contains lines of written information that can be sent direct to a screen or printer by using ordinary **operating system** commands. The files produced by word processors are normally not text files. Although they contain text, they also contain special **codes** that are not usually displayed on the screen but govern important **formatting functions** such as margins, underlining, and so on. The meaning of these codes is special to the word processing software being used. Most word processors can, however, produce text files and provide an option for this under the *File Save As* menu.

KEY POINT

A simple text file made of numbers and or letters consists of the code for each character in the file. The ASCII character code is normally used. It does not contain any special command or formatting codes, but end of line markers do have their own ASCII code, so they are included. Files are often converted into simple ASCII code when they are to be transferred from one information system to another because most software packages are able to read ASCII code.

PROGRESS CHECK

1. Why is code sometimes used to enter data into an information system?
2. What are the important points to remember if you are designing a code?
3. What is a key field?

3. The term used to describe a field that is unique to a particular record and that can therefore be used to search a file to locate the record quickly.
2. A code must be easy to use. It should be easy to remember, and not too long or complicated. Codes must not be too short either and should always be the same length. This provides an easy way of performing a validation check on them.
1. Code may be used for one, or a combination of, three main reasons. Codes can be input more quickly, and make searches faster too. Using codes reduces the size of files, so that data processing is faster.

Sample GCSE questions

1 Describe one difference between a Local Area Network (LAN) and a Wide Area Network (WAN).

> *A LAN is normally within one room or building while a WAN is spread over long distances (e.g. Internet).* **[2]**

Where there are only 2 marks for a question with two answers, the examiner will only be looking for you to state your answer. If there are more marks for your answer they will want you to expand on the answer and give examples.

2 The name given to the ways computer networks are connected together is topology. Name each of the topologies shown below.

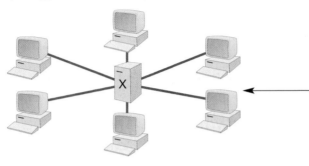

If you don't know the answer to this type of question try to guess it using network terms. You may get a mark for using the correct terminology.

Name of topology   *Star network* **[1]**

What is the name given to the computer in Position X?

> *Server or central processing unit.* **[1]**

Name of topology   *Line network* **[1]**

Draw a hierarchical network.

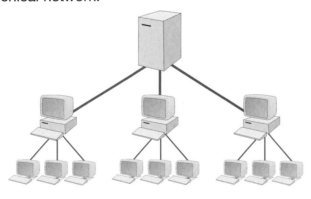

[2]

3 The database below is part of a shop's customer file.

Reference	Surname	First name	Gender	Address	Postcode
001	Patel	Sanjay	M	12, Willis Way	MM12 6BS
002	Smith	Eleanor	F	37, Holme Close	MM12 7HR
003	Buzan	Pierre	M	95, Whinbush Walk	MM11 3QV
004	Brady	Maureen	F	61, Fairbank Gardens	MM9 4PC

Sample GCSE questions

(a) How many records are shown on the database?

4

[1]

(b) For each record, how many fields are shown?

6

[1]

(c) The column labelled Gender uses codes. Give three reasons why the shop would wish to use codes in this column.

One   *codes are quicker to key in*

Two   *less storage space required*

Three   *easy to validate*

[3]

(d) State the name of a field that contains numeric data.

Reference field

[1]

> You will need to use the correct terminology in this type of question to get the marks.

(e) Give the name of a field that uses alphanumeric data.

Postcode field

[1]

(f) The Reference column is used as a key field. What is a key field?

A field that is unique to a record, used only once, and can be used to locate that record quickly.

[3]

4 On the chart below, tick two applications that use real-time processing.

> Only tick the number of boxes you are asked to tick. You will lose marks for ticking more boxes.

Printing examination certificates	
Calculating electricity bills	
Central heating system	✔
Sending out reminders for overdue books	
Automatic pilot on an aeroplane	✔
Clearing cheques in a bank	

On the chart below, tick two applications that use batch processing.

Monitoring a patient's pulse rate	
Producing gas bills	✔
Air traffic control system	
On-line cinema seat reservation system	
Clearing cheques in a bank	✔
Recording wind speed in an experiment	

[2]

Sample GCSE questions

5   Compare the relative advantages and disadvantages of email and fax communication to send data and information around the world.

Example answer:

Advantages of email: fast communication to any destination; can send large documents very quickly; is inexpensive if properly used (local telephone call rates).

Disadvantages: user must have access to and connect to computer to get messages; not all users have email; certain security risks; original documents cannot be sent; viruses may attach to emails.

Advantages of fax: more secure way of sending financial details; data not saved on intermediate computers.

Disadvantages: paper required and receiving machine may not be loaded with paper; not everyone has a fax machine; cannot send original material.   **[10]**

> *This type of question wants you to contrast advantages with disadvantages. Try to fill all the answer lines with a reasoned argument. Use correct terminology wherever possible. Don't forget to give both advantages and disadvantages.*

6   **(a)**   What would you use to look for video suppliers on the Internet?
1.   a fax   ☐
2.   a CD-ROM   ☐
3.   a spreadsheet   ☐
4.   a search engine   ☑   **[2]**

> *The Key Skill tests and some examination papers make use of multiple choice questions. Tick only one answer and think carefully before you answer.*

(b)   To send an email to your friends you need a connection to a
1.   search engine   ☐
2.   telephone network   ☑
3.   scanner   ☐
4.   printer   ☐   **[1]**

Exam practice questions

1 Explain what a Local Area network is and list briefly its advantages and disadvantages.

....

....

....

....

.... **[12]**

2 Name and explain the main features of the four commonest ways of laying out a network.

....

....

....

....

.... **[5]**

3 Explain briefly how the World Wide Web is used.

....

....

....

....

.... **[6]**

4 Outline how you would use a search engine to find information on the World Wide Web.

....

....

....

....

.... **[4]**

Exam practice questions

5 In Internet terms, what is the meaning of the term protocols?

....

....

....

....

.... **[6]**

6 Explain briefly how email works.

....

....

....

....

.... **[6]**

7 Discuss advantages of using email and the World Wide Web.

....

....

....

....

.... **[6]**

8 Outline the structures that organise data stored in an information system.

....

....

....

....

.... **[6]**

9 Describe how information systems can be linked together on a world-wide scale.

....

....

....

....

.... **[4]**

- any constraints on the system – limitations on solutions to perceived problems. A constraint might be the amount of space available, or finance available
- an update of cost/benefit analysis based on the new information

As long as the **feasibility** report does recommend that a new system will be an improvement on the old one, further **analysis** will be carried out to determine exactly what the new system has to be able to do.

Requirement specification

OCR A   OCR B
EDEXCEL
AQA A   AQA B
NICCEA

A **requirement specification** will be produced and will detail all of the **inputs** that will have to be produced, and all special user requirements also. Responsibilities of members of the team involved with the project will be set out, with **deadlines** by which stages must be completed.

For example, a user may want a system to be developed using a particular database package, with ability to store and manipulate pictures. If the package will not allow the manipulation of pictures, it means that the requirements conflict.

KEY POINT

> The **requirement specification** will form the basis for later stages in developing the system and must therefore be detailed. The people using the existing system must be able to understand it, and it must be checked with users to make sure that the new system will do everything that is required. It must also be checked to ensure that there are no **conflicts** in the list of requirements.

Users can be unrealistic about what can be achieved in a new system and the requirement specification must ensure that all hardware and software proposed is capable of performing the tasks required.

The requirement specification can be used later to check that the new system is being put together properly, and it can be used as the basis for evaluation of the completed system.

Design

OCR A   OCR B
EDEXCEL
AQA A   AQA B
NICCEA
WJEC

As more computers are added to a system, more maintenance is required.

The system must now be designed to meet the **requirement specification**. It is often useful to break down a large system into **subsystems** that are easier to work with.

A supermarket information system, for example, might be divided into:

- customer section – scanning of items purchased, production of customer receipts, taking care of customer store card information
- banking section – accepting payment from customers and corresponding with banks to obtain direct payment when debit cards are used, and payment when credit cards or cheques are used. Updating store and central accounts
- stock control – monitoring information about stock moving in and out of the store. Ordering stock whenever needed. Providing information about levels of sales

A **structure diagram** can be produced to show how the subsystems fit together to make the whole system.

In the design stage, it is very important to think about the way each part of the **system** interacts with its users. This **human user interface** should be consistent throughout the system. The following points might be considered:

- **Use of colour**. Colour can be useful to highlight messages, but too many colours can be confusing. There should always be good contrast between colours so that words are readable and images clear. Red is often considered to be a warning colour, so might be kept for warning messages. The designer must bear in mind that some users may be colour blind so it will be best to avoid combining red and green or blue and yellow.

- **Sound**. Sound should be reserved for situations where it is essential. Music systems require sound, of course, but it would be a distraction in an accounts system. Warning sounds can be used, and sound may be useful in certain situations, for example bar code readers in supermarkets normally bleep to indicate correct reading.

- **Flashing symbols**. These can be used to attract user attention, but the designer must be aware that certain flash rates can cause epileptic fits, and flashing symbols can be distracting and annoying.

- **Location of items on the screen**. The designer will try to keep the same items in the same place on all screens forming part of the system. This will make the system easier to use. Users tend to look mostly at the top third of a screen and important messages like error messages may not be seen if they are placed at the bottom of a screen.

- **Movement from screen to screen**. The designer should make sure that the same method is always used to move between screens. It is irritating for users if some screens need just a key-press when others need a specific word, followed by the enter key.

- **Making choices**. The designer should also make sure that the same method is always used where users have to indicate that they have made a choice. The input device used is likely to be the mouse or the keyboard, but should not be a mixture of the two. Lack of continuity makes the system much harder to learn.

- **Appropriate use of language**. The designer will make sure that the type of language used is suitable for the users of the system. Graphics may work better than words in some cases.

System design

As the outputs of a system often affect how the **system functions**, **outputs** are usually examined first.

Outputs

Outputs can take many forms and may include:

- an invoice, receipt or bill
- a dispatch note
- a packing slip
- a screen display
- a sound

Before the system can be designed it is important that the type of output is considered. Frequency and volume of the output must also be taken into account. Refer back to the section on inputs, processing and outputs.

Inputs

Once the type of output has been established the type and method of **capturing** the data needs to be considered.
Inputs can consist of:

- numerical data
- pictures
- sounds
- text
- movement

Again the frequency and volume of input needs careful consideration before the input device can be selected. Diagrams are a good way to represent the inputs and outputs of your system.

Data preparation

Data preparation will involve getting **raw data** into a form that can be **processed** by the new system.

> **KEY POINT**
> Techniques for verification and validation form part of data preparation. Verification involves making sure that, if a keyboard has been used, no typing mistakes or other data entry errors have been made.

Various validation methods can be used to trap errors and this will be carried out by system software.

Code design

The new system may use **codes** to save data entry time and storage space. Codes must be carefully designed if they are to be useful. There is no point in designing codes that users will find impossible to remember.

File design

The designer has to know how many **files** are needed, and then to design the structure of each of the files. He or she will take care not to duplicate any information.

Hardware configuration

The most appropriate **hardware devices** must be chosen and, if more than one computer will be used, the **network topology** must also be designed.

The description of what must be done is known as an algorithm.

There are various ways of describing algorithms, including flow charts, structure diagrams and pseudocode. Pseudocode is an outline of a computer program written in a mixture of programming language and English. It is one of the best ways of planning a computer program.

Software

The processing that the system has to do must be designed. **Processes** may include searching, sorting, performing calculations or producing text or graphics. If the solution is based on an existing package such as a spreadsheet or database package, it will be possible to produce simple descriptions of what must be done and the software will do most of the work.

> **KEY POINT**
> Where a suitable package is not already available, it will be necessary to write a more detailed algorithm to explain how the program will work.
> - An algorithm is a sequence of instructions that tell how to solve a particular problem. An algorithm must be specified exactly, so that there can be no doubt about what to do next, and it must have a finite number of steps. A computer program is an algorithm written in a language that a computer can understand (see page 52).
> - The same algorithm can be written in different languages.

Testing

OCR A   OCR B
EDEXCEL
AQA A   AQA B
NICCEA
WJEC

It is important that a new system is thoroughly **tested** before it is introduced. Test data to be used in this process will have been **devised during the design stage** and testing is carried out regularly throughout implementation of a system. The general principle of testing is to check that the system works properly with typical data, data at the limits of what is allowed (extreme data), and data that is wrong.

> **KEY POINT**
>
> It is also necessary to check that the system meets all of the requirements set out in the requirements specification, and that it will be acceptable to the users. The testing of the system can be broken down into five stages:
> 1. The system is tested with data that contains no errors to see if it produces the correct results.
> 2. The system is tested with data that contains errors to see how this data will be processed. Ideally, all the errors will be picked up by validation procedures but it is impossible for the computer to detect every type of error.
> 3. The system is tested with very large volumes of data to see if it can handle this, and if it might be able to cope with increased work in future.
> 4. System processes that are required only occasionally are tested. An example might be the production of a salary report on a certain day of the month.
> 5. Extreme data is entered into the system to test how this is processed. The range checks included in the validation program should detect any unsuitable data.

You will be expected to test your own system as part of your coursework. The exam paper may ask you to list checks that could be carried out to check a system.

If the results of all tests are positive, the system can be introduced, or implemented.

Implementation

OCR A   OCR B
EDEXCEL
AQA A   AQA B
NICCEA
WJEC

During this stage, the **hardware** and **software** that have been selected are installed in their working positions, and set to produce the required outputs.

It is common for a large new system to be **implemented** in **stages**, with the most important sections being installed first. As each section is implemented, it will be tested thoroughly and when the entire new system is complete, a full system test will be carried out.

> **KEY POINT**
>
> There are three common ways of installing systems in organisations: direct implementation, phased implementation and parallel running.

Direct implementation

This method is normally used only where a small system is being implemented. All of the users begin to use the system on a certain date. The method is quick and simple where no problems occur. It is not so suitable for larger systems because, despite testing, problems do often occur in the early stages of implementation and if all users tried to switch at the same time, there could be chaos.

Phased implementation

You may be asked to say which method you would use and the advantages of your chosen method over the other two.

This method introduces each task separately and ensures that it is running smoothly before another task is brought into the **system**. For instance, in the supermarket example, the stock control section might be implemented first. Disadvantages are that implementation takes much longer, and benefits of the new system are delayed.

Parallel running

In this method the new system is started and **run alongside** the old system, which can act as a backup if problems develop with the new system. Results from the new system can be compared with results from the old system. However, since each job is carried out twice, there is more work for users and each job will take twice as long.

Documentation

If you cannot remember the terms try to think through who the end users will be and what their needs are. Someone will need to maintain the system. Someone will use the system.

Documentation of a system is very important and is likely to be divided into two distinct types. People who use the system every day will need clear instructions to get the best results from it, but they do not really need to know how the system works.

They will need **user documentation**.

People responsible for maintaining the system do need to know how the system works, and may have to adapt the system as user needs change.

They need **technical documentation**.

User documentation

This will usually take the form of a user guide or manual that users can turn to when they need to learn new procedures, or deal with problems that arise.

KEY POINT

A user guide should cover points such as:
- how to load the software
- how to perform everyday functions
- how to save
- how to print

The various jobs that the system can do should be described in a logical order in a user guide.

Illustrations may be used to help explanations, and the guide may include examples and exercises to help users become familiar with the new system. It should have a contents page and an index to help users find the answers to their questions, and a glossary that explains any new terms may be useful.

It should tell users what to do in exceptional circumstances. For example, if data is sent to a printer when the printer is not switched on, the user will need to know what steps to follow. However, the user guide will not provide technical details that are not needed for everyday use of the system.

Technical documentation

This will explain the system to the **programmers** and **systems analysts** who will be responsible for maintaining and possibly adapting the system.

> **KEY POINT**
>
> The documentation will be written in precise technical language and will include test data and the results of testing. In the longer term, it may be invaluable to explain the working of the system to a new expert who was not around when the system was implemented. Like the user documentation, technical documentation also requires a contents page and comprehensive index.

Evaluation

OCR A   OCR B
EDEXCEL
AQA A   AQA B
NICCEA
WJEC

A **full evaluation** of a new system is carried out when it is all installed and running.

The evaluation will be based on criteria set by looking at the requirement specification that was produced at the end of the **analysis stage**.

> **KEY POINT**
>
> A full evaluation will demand detailed answers to a range of questions designed to determine whether the system carries out all required tasks properly, and how well it achieves each task. A scoring system may be useful in a full evaluation, and it may indicate areas where changes will be needed.

It is important to ensure that you have a good specification before designing the system. This gives you a good starting point for an evaluation.

Be careful not to write too much detail in an examination. The number of lines given for your answer will help to guide you as to the amount you should write.

As the system and its users settle into **regular use**, evaluation sessions are likely to be carried out at **regular intervals**. Users of the system will always be consulted in such evaluations and they are the people who will be aware of any problems.

Present constraints such as time, money or numbers of qualified staff may be looked at with a view to making improvements in future.

Maintenance

OCR A   OCR B
EDEXCEL
AQA A   AQA B
WJEC

All systems need **maintenance** to keep them running properly. Commercial software is often upgraded for this reason. There are three main reasons why information systems need maintenance.

Corrective maintenance

This is the type of maintenance needed to **fix problems** that show up once the system is in use. Careful testing before full implementation should minimise the number and scope of such problems, but it is impossible to create a system that is perfect.

Adaptive maintenance

This type of maintenance makes changes in the system to suit variations or growth in requirements once it is in use. For example, if a supermarket wanted to link its store card scheme to a reward scheme such as Air Miles, its information system would have to be changed accordingly.

Perfective maintenance

This type of maintenance makes the system better than it was in the first place. The supermarket's managers, for example, might decide that they want to send a newsletter every three months to every customer who buys above a certain value of goods in the store. The newsletter would carry promotions and special offers, and the supermarket's information system would be modified to cope with this demand.

Evaluation and maintenance will continue throughout the life time of an information system. A stage is likely to be reached eventually where so many improvements or repairs are needed that it is better to build a new system. At this point the life cycle starts all over again.

PROGRESS CHECK

1. What is meant by the life cycle of a system?
2. Explain the function of a feasibility report.
3. Explain briefly why it is necessary to have two different types of documentation with a system.

1. It describes the series of stages that any information system goes through, from initial conception and design, through the months or years of its use, to the time when so many improvements or repairs are needed that it is better to design a new system.
2. In systems analysis, a feasibility report explains whether a new system would be better than the existing system, and gives reasons. It outlines what could be achieved with a new system.
3. Technical documentation is required for those involved in the building and maintenance of the system. They must understand exactly how it works. User documentation is required for the people who use the system each day. They need to know how to achieve the functions required in their jobs, but do not need to understand technical details.

Sample GCSE questions

1 A new system is to be introduced into a school for pupils to pay for their dinner using computer cards. Describe the steps that will be taken in the analysis and design of this new system.

Example answer:

Carry out research on the current situation; analyse the output required; work out what information the new system needs; analyse processing required; analyse the constraints of the system – cost, time; break the task down into achievable steps; estimate resources required; produce a diagram of the solution (block diagram or system flowchart); design appropriate methods of data capture; design internal organisation of data; select appropriate hardware; select appropriate software; observation of current system; obtain opinions of those who will run and use the system; look at current documentation; plan appropriate documentation of new system; use of questionnaires; look at corresponding system in another school; design screen displays. **[6]**

> Try to explain the process in clear logical stages. You can draw upon the knowledge you will have gained designing a system yourself.

2 When a system is tested, what are the five stages normally followed?

First the system is tested with data that contains no errors to see if it produces the correct results.

Then it is tested with data that contains errors to see how this data will be processed. It will be impossible for the computer to detect every type of error.

Thirdly the system is tested with very large volumes of data to see if it can handle this, and if it might be able to cope with increased work in future.

System processes that are required only occasionally are then tested. Finally, data that is known to be close to or outside the range of the system is entered to see how this is processed. The range checks included in the validation program should detect any unsuitable data. **[6]**

> If you are asked for a number of stages think through which are the most important.

3 A school plans to introduce a computerised system for attendance registers. The system will make each pupil responsible for registering that he or she is present each school day. This will be monitored by school staff.

(a) Give details of five points that might be included in a feasibility report that is produced during analysis for the school.

> A number of exam papers ask questions based upon school ICT systems. Try to find out about the systems in use in your school including the administration systems.

Sample GCSE questions

Examples:

One   *how well the existing system functions*

Two   *cost in time and money terms of existing system*

Three *attitudes to existing system - staff and pupils*

Four   *cost in time and money of installing new system*

Five   *attitudes to proposed new system, in particular to pupils having*
responsibility for their own attendance tracking   **[5]**

(b)   List three points that should be taken into consideration when
designing the human interface for the new system.

Examples:

One   *use of colour or sound*

Two   *any flashing symbols*

Three *location of items on the screen*   **[3]**

(c)   Describe the types of user documentation that will be required
to help the new system run efficiently.

Examples:

Technical documentation will be required for maintenance
staff who will keep the system running properly and make
any required changes to it; user documentation will be
required specifically for both staff and pupils so that each
group knows how to use their aspect of the new system.   **[4]**

*Remember the two types
of user for your system:
the teachers/pupils and
the technician.*

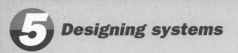

Exam practice questions

1   Outline briefly what happens at each stage in a system life cycle.

    ....
    ....
    ....
    ....
    ....
    ....
    ....
    .... **[12]**

2   What methods might be used to evaluate an existing system?

    ....
    ....
    ....
    ....
    .... **[8]**

3   Design of the new human interface is very important for a new system.
    What points should be taken into consideration?

    ....
    ....
    ....
    ....
    .... **[4]**

The following topics are covered in this chapter:

- 6.1 Security of systems and data
- 6.2 Passwords, encryption and backups
- 6.3 Data quality
- 6.4 Misuse of data

6.1 Security of systems and data

After completing this section you should be able to:

LEARNING SUMMARY

- explain why security is important to an information system and its users
- suggest typical consequences of data loss
- discuss the physical threats to system security, including deliberate damage and theft
- list measures that can be taken to guard against theft
- discuss 'internal' threats to systems and applications software – viruses
- list precautions to guard against viruses
- discuss how data loss can occur as a result of accidental damage or computer failure

> Questions on security are common. They can take two forms, asking you to say how you could make data secure or asking why an end user, e.g. a doctor or patient, would be concerned about private information being held on a computer.

It is very important to keep information systems as **secure** as possible. The **hardware** and **software** that make up a system are expensive to buy, and the **data** and **information** that form the heart of the system have even greater value.

KEY POINT

Much data is of a confidential nature. It can be politically sensitive, or dangerous in the wrong hands. A lot of the data entered into an information system may be irreplaceable if it is the result of tests or surveys that would have different results if they were repeated.

> The cost of creating data again from scratch can far outweigh the cost of replacing hardware or software.

The loss of data from a business information system could have a number of consequences, such as:

- cash flow problems, which could cause a struggling business to go bankrupt
- making bad business decisions, because they are based on incomplete or incorrect information

- failure to receive or make payments at the correct time
- late or non-delivery of goods to purchasers
- loss of goodwill from customers
- bad publicity from news media

In a different context, such as a hospital, data loss could have results that could threaten the lives of patients. For example, if a record of a patient's allergies was lost, the patient might be dosed with a drug that he or she was allergic to. Loss of data on a Police information system might lead to the wrong person being accused of a crime.

A number of types of threat can endanger the security of an information system and its data.

Physical threats

The equipment that forms an information system, and its data, needs **physical security**.

Hazards include natural ones such as fire, lightning and water damage, and can also include deliberate damage or theft.

Protection from fires

Fire can be caused by an outside agent such as lightning or a faulty electrical system. It may be caused deliberately by an arsonist, or it may originate from computer hardware itself.

Computers themselves do not often catch fire, however. A more frequent cause is faulty wiring or overloaded electrical sockets. Many large computer rooms and offices are fitted with smoke detectors, and fire doors can help stop fires spreading. Gas flooding systems are used in large computer installations. These are preferred to water sprinkling systems because the water can often do more damage than the fire.

 KEY POINT Back-up copies should be kept in containers that are fire and heat proof. Metal containers heat up in a fire, and the tapes and disks they contain will then melt and be useless.

Protection from dust and extremes of temperature

Large mainframe computers create a lot of heat, and temperature and humidity in rooms housing mainframes are controlled by air conditioning systems. Air is also filtered before it enters these rooms.

 KEY POINT Vital components such as the hard drive of a computer, which uses dust-sensitive disks, are sealed inside the computer. External data storage media such as CDs and floppy disks are kept in plastic covers to protect them from dust and scratching.

Computer theft

Methods such as keyboard locks and passwords can be used to make sure that unauthorised people do not gain access to a system, but that does not stop a thief picking up the hardware itself and stealing it.

> **KEY POINT**
>
> Hardware can be protected by means of locks, bolts, clamps, alarmed circuits and tags. It is often easier to make sure that the room and building in which the equipment is housed is secure. If a building is secure, any computer hardware in it is more likely to be secure too. Buildings can be fitted with sophisticated intruder alarms. Staff and visitors can use security badges, and individual rooms can be fitted with keypad locks.

Various other measures can be used to help prevent computer theft:

- A record should be made of all the **serial numbers** of computers and **peripherals**. This record must be kept in a secure place, and may provide police with a way of identifying stolen equipment.

- With some computers, it is possible to lock the case of the computer. This prevents it being turned on. The case should be locked whenever the computer is not in use, and the key kept in a secure place.

- Data must be backed-up regularly on to an external storage medium, which is kept in a secure place, away from the computer. If the hardware itself if stolen, at least the data is not lost. However, the data held in the stolen computer can still be used by the thieves, unless it has been **encrypted** (see below).

> **You will not need to know about specific viruses but you should understand what a virus is and how you can protect a system from one.**

- All those working in or using a building where there are computers should be made aware of security, and encouraged to question any suspicious behaviour.

- If an ID badge system is used, it is important that everyone in a building, regardless of their status, wears a badge. This gives out a message that the organisation is security conscious.

Viruses

OCR A **OCR B**
EDEXCEL
AQA A **AQA B**
WJEC
Key Skills

Apart from the physical threats described above, the main danger to software is probably that of **viruses**.

> **KEY POINT**
>
> A virus is a computer program that automatically copies itself so that it can 'infect' other disks or programs without the user's knowledge. It is then capable of playing some kind of trick, or of disrupting the operation of the computer.

> **E-commerce is only possible with secure communications.**

Viruses were first written as practical jokes, but it is all too common now for them to be written by people who wish to cause **malicious damage** to information systems. Because of the virus's ability to copy itself, the scale of the damage can be serious and widespread. Viruses are quite common, and some have become well known to systems users, who have developed methods of dealing with them.

> **Some exam questions ask what damage a virus can cause, others how to protect a system from one.**

Most systems use **antivirus** software to guard against damage by viruses. The software is able to scan through the memory and disks of a computer to detect the presence of any viruses. It can then remove them, in a process that is sometimes called **disinfecting**. When choosing antivirus software, it is important to compare speeds of checking and buy a package that is suitable for your system.

Users of any computer system can take regular precautions against the threat of viruses:

- Obtain all software from a reliable source.

- If you do buy second-hand software, scan it for viruses first.

- Make regular back-up copies of work.

- Write-protect any external disks that relate to the operating system or that contain data that must not be altered. A floppy or zip disk has a tiny write-protect tab in one corner. If you can see through the hole by this tab, you will not be able to write to the disk. (If you close the hole by moving the tab across it, you will be able to read and write data.) CD-ROMs and CD-Rs are automatically write-protected. Files on a CD-RW, or any other files, can be protected by saving them in Read-only format. Files can also be protected with passwords. It is important to remember that files that have been protected with passwords, for example, are no longer protected if you, as the legitimate user, enter the password and open the file.

- Run antivirus software at regular intervals. Most systems are set up so that this software runs automatically when a computer is switched on. It should also check external disks before data is taken from them.

- If a computer has had to be repaired, it should be scanned for viruses before being used again.

- Be wary of downloading software from bulletin boards. They provide one of the easiest ways for people who write viruses to spread them around.

- Be suspicious of all software distributed free of charge. Examples are software and **shareware** (software that is copyrighted but can be distributed free of charge. Users are asked or required to make a payment direct to the author if they use the program regularly) which are distributed in magazines. These sometimes carry viruses.

> Some exam questions are structured so that the answer to the question is to protect the system from a virus, e.g. why should you not let someone use your computer from a floppy disk without checking it first?

Data loss

OCR A OCR B
EDEXCEL
AQA A AQA B
NICCEA
WJEC

The main cause of data loss is **accidental damage**. It most often results from carelessness by systems users. People may get dirt on disks and tapes, for example, and this will not only damage the data stored on them, but may also damage the drive into which they are inserted.

Also, computers are not infallible. They can develop problems, particularly if overloaded with software, or if they are nearing the end of their **working life**.

> Sudden, unexpected power failures can also lead to loss of data that has not been saved.

KEY POINT

> The reliability of a computer, like that of many other machines, is measured in terms of mean time between failure. A typical hard disk unit has a mean time between failures of between 20,000 to 200,000 hours. If it is part of a network, the failure of an individual computer may affect the whole network. Systems failures can thus cause the loss of large numbers of important files.

Data loss can also be caused when a user is not **familiar** with a system or particular software, and is not sure what to do next, or makes mistakes with **commands** or other interactions with the system. For this reason, it is important to limit access to a computer's operating system, particularly for inexperienced users.

Restricted access can also be used to prevent people from copying data from the hard disk to a floppy or CD.

Stand-alone computers are usually safe because there is no connection for hackers to break into. Computers that form part of networks, or those with external links (Internet access is the most common) are in danger from hackers.

A simple **command** at the **operating systems prompt** could erase an entire hard disk.

Unfortunately, **deliberate damage** to files is most often caused by the employees of a business, and the worst damage can be caused by those who have the highest level of access to the system. This is why, when staff working at this level have to be dismissed, they are not allowed to go near the computer system.

Carelessness such as leaving a screen displaying important and sensitive information can be a source of too much temptation for some. It is then easy to **change** or **delete** data. However, data is most often stolen by employees or in situations where a large system is shared by several companies.

KEY POINT

- Data theft can happen as a result of people hacking into a computer system.
- A hacker is a person who breaks codes and passwords to gain access to computers without authorisation, either for malicious reasons, or just to prove it can be done.

PROGRESS CHECK

1. Why is security important to an information system, and to its users?
2. What may happen if data is lost?
3. What type of physical threats does system security face?
4. What can be done to try to prevent computer theft?
5. Describe the principal 'internal' threat to systems and applications software.
6. How do viruses infect a computer system?
7. What precautions can be taken to guard against viruses?
8. How can accidental damage or computer failure lead to loss of data?

1. Much data is of a confidential nature and must be protected from falling into the wrong hands. A lot of the data entered into an information system may be irreplaceable. The cost of creating data again from scratch can far outweigh the cost of replacing hardware or software.
2. A company could experience serious cash flow problems, its managers might make bad business decisions, because they are based on incomplete or incorrect information; payments might not be made or demanded at the right time; goods might be delivered late to customers. A hospital or dentist might give the wrong treatment to patients.
3. Physical threats include fire – deliberate or accidental, water damage, damage by extremes of temperature, dust damage, deliberate damage by users, and theft.
4. Ensure that the building where all computer equipment is housed is secure. Alarms, an ID badge system for all staff, and staff awareness campaigns can help. Serial numbers of all equipment should be recorded and all data backed up and backups stored in a different place.
5. Computer viruses are small programs that 'hijack' a computer and use it to reproduce and spread themselves in the same way as viruses can spread in a human body.
6. Viruses attach themselves to computer programs and data files. They can then spread without the user's knowledge by copying themselves on to floppy disks, then on to other hard disks and also across networks.
7. It is best to use reliable software always, and to run antivirus software regularly. Data should be backed up regularly and important disks write-protected. Any computer that has been repaired, or any software received second-hand should always be scanned for viruses before use. Be wary of software from bulletin boards and freeware.
8. With high level of use, computer systems are likely to develop faults that can cause the loss of quantities of data, as can inexperienced human users who are unfamiliar with software and do not know the correct procedures to use.

6.2 Passwords, encryption and back-ups

LEARNING SUMMARY

After completing this section you should be able to:

- *describe why and how passwords and IDs are used with information systems*
- *explain the process of encryption and its purpose*
- *explain the importance of backing up files*
- *list general rules for backing up files*

Passwords and ID

OCR A OCR B
EDEXCEL
AQA A AQA B
WJEC
Key Skills

****___

Passwords can be used to protect files against damage or theft, in the same way as they are used to **protect against viruses**. Individual system users can also be allocated **Ids** and **passwords** that allow them a particular **level of access** to the system.

For example, an accounts clerk might have an ID, which might be a word of some sort, and a password allowing access to files needed to check invoices, while a finance director would have access to all accounts files.

Examiners sometimes ask questions about how to secure data for different levels of access. Passwords are the key to answering this type of question.

 KEY POINT

When setting up password systems it is best to use numeric or alphanumeric codes, **and these should be reasonably long. It takes much longer to try all possible combinations of letters and numbers to crack a six-character code, than for a three-character code. It is best to avoid real words because these can sometimes be guessed easily. Ids and passwords should never be written down and left near the computer.**

Encryption

OCR A OCR B
EDEXCEL
AQA A AQA B
WJEC

Encryption can be performed automatically.

Files containing sensitive data can be **protected** by codes in a process called **encryption**. If a tape or disk containing **encrypted files** is stolen, it would be impossible to read it without a **decoder**.

Encryption is used when **important data** is being transmitted from one place to another. The data is coded by the **source computer** before being sent, and **decoded** at the destination computer. The processes are performed

When people are using credit or debit cards to pay for goods bought via the Internet, the card details are always encrypted.

automatically by the computers involved. If the data is intercepted en route, it cannot be **interpreted** or altered.

Encryption can also be used with **emails** to make sure that they reach the right destination, and are not intercepted on the way.

Encryption ensures privacy for the sender and recipient of a message, but some governments are not in favour of encryption of emails. They believe that it encourages crime by making it easy for those who want to break the law to communicate with each other.

You do not need to know how to encrypt data but will be expected to know when to encrypt data and describe who may use encryption, e.g. banks etc.

Backing-up data

OCR A   OCR B
EDEXCEL
WJEC
Key Skills

Backing-up data means taking a copy of the data and keeping it away from the computer in a safe place. Both operating system programs and **user files** should be backed-up. This straightforward measure helps to **protect** against **accidental** or **deliberate data loss**, or theft of data.

Backing-up data regularly is vitally important. It guards against power cuts, theft and systems failures.

It is possible to use specialised software capable of retrieving lost files, but this does not always work successfully, and is no substitute for making regular back-up files.

KEY POINT

There are some general rules that should be observed when storing back-ups:
- Never keep back-up disks near the computer. If the computer is stolen, the thief is likely to take the disks as well, particularly if they are in an obvious place, like a desk drawer.
- If a lot of important data is to be held on back-up copies, it is worth buying a fire-proof safe in which to keep the disks or tapes.
- In a large organisation, it is worth keeping at least one set of back-up disks or tapes on a different site.

1. Why are passwords used with information systems, and how are they used?
2. What is meant by encryption?
3. What is the encryption used for?
4. Why is it important to back up files?
5. What are the rules to remember when storing backed up files?

PROGRESS CHECK

1. As part of system security measures to make sure that only authorised users have access to certain areas of systems.
2. The process of converting information into a code so that people will be unable to read it, unless they have an appropriate key to the code.
3. To protect sensitive data such as financial information sent over networks, and email messages, so that they can be sent from a secure source to a secure destination without anyone else being able to read them on the way.
4. Regular back-up of files helps to protect against accidental or deliberate data loss, and theft. It guards against sudden power cuts and computer breakdowns.
5. Back-ups should be kept well away from the source computer, ideally in a different room, and in a fire-proof place. Most large organisations keep one copy of vital back-ups in a completely different location.

6.3 *Data quality*

After completing this section you should be able to:

● *describe the two methods of checking data on input – verification checks and validation checks*
● *suggest why data accuracy is important*
● *discuss the question of whether all information that derives from an information system is true*
● *describe a basic data logging system*
● *describe in detail the considerations that might govern the choice of a type of output – both in terms of audience, and equipment available*
● *discuss and compare the main types of output from an information system: printed output, screen output, multimedia output, sound output and virtual reality*

Checking data on input

OCR A   OCR B
EDEXCEL
AQA A   AQA B
WJEC

> There are various ways of carrying out a verification check. Some exam questions ask you to identify them.

Data has to be checked when it is entered into a computer system. Two types of checking – **verification** and **validation** – are carried out (page 113).

Verification checks

A **verification check** makes sure that data that has been entered, or copied from another medium, has been **transferred** correctly.

● Sometimes, where data is to be entered via a keyboard, two operators may be asked to enter the same data. The two versions can then be compared and, if they match, the data is stored. If not, the source document is looked at to see where mistakes are. Any mistakes can then be corrected and stored. This type of verification check is time consuming because two people are required to do one job.

● One simple way of trying to verify input data is to display it on the screen and ask the operator who has entered it to read it through and indicate if it is correct. Unfortunately, operators often do not see their own mistakes, or do not believe that they have made any mistakes and therefore do not even read through the data before confirming it is correct.

● A parity check makes use of the binary code understood by the computer to try to make sure that data is not corrupted during transfer. When groups of bits (1s and 0s) are being transferred, an extra bit is added so that the total number of 1s is always odd (or, alternatively, always even). This is called the parity of the data.

● One incorrectly transmitted bit will change the parity, making it possible to detect the error. However, if an even number of incorrect bits has been transmitted, the parity is not changed. Even though not all errors are detected, the user is warned by those that are indicated and can check the data more thoroughly to locate others.

Validation checks

Validation checking is carried out by the **software** to make sure that data is sensible and will not cause problems when it is processed.

> **KEY POINT**
>
> - Type checks make sure that numerical data does not accidentally contain letters. For example, an accidental letter 'O' in place of a zero would be noticed.
> - A range check is used to make sure that data is inside a fixed set of values. For example, prices might have to be between 50p and £9.99. A range check can be used with letters as well as numbers. A set range of letters can be specified. For example, authors of books on one shelf rack in a library might have names beginning with any letter from N to S.
> - A presence check makes sure that a value has actually been entered in a particular field. This type of check is used where certain vital data must be entered. An example would be a patient's blood group where a hospital has to give a blood transfusion.

Check digits are used widely to **validate numeric** data, especially where numbers with many digits are being entered.

The check digit is a single digit number calculated from all the rest of the digits in a data item and then attached to the end of the data when it is stored.

There is a check digit in the ISBN on a book. They can be used to detect **transposition errors**, when two digits are entered the wrong way round, and changes or losses of digits in numbers. When an operator inputs the number, the check digit is recalculated and the two versions are compared. If they match, the data is correct and can be saved. If they do not match, there is a mistake and the number has to be re-input.

Quality of data

OCR A   OCR B
EDEXCEL
AQA A   AQA B
WJEC

It is important to remember that although **verification checks** will attempt to ensure that data is copied correctly, and **validation checks** will pinpoint data that has numerical or character errors, there is no way of making sure that the data entered into a computer system is either accurate or true.

Nobody has yet written software that can act as a **lie detector**. It is up to the user to make sure that **data entered** is **accurate**, otherwise **outputs** from the system will be wrong.

It is true that if you put rubbish in, you will get rubbish out.

The question of **truth** is a difficult one, particularly in relation to the **Internet**. Web pages are innocently used by thousands of people as **electronic reference books**, but there is no check on the quality of the information displayed on them. The user can only hope that, if the site is provided by a reputable organisation, the information offered can be believed (see disadvantages of Internet and email, page 101).

Data logging and control technology

EDEXCEL
OCR A OCR B
WJEC

(See also pages 69 and 70.)

Data logging is the term for the automatic recording of data as it is produced. The capture and storage of data for a data logging system is called data acquisition.

Exam questions sometimes ask you to state the requirements of a data logging system to perform a given experiment.

For example, in a weather station, temperature may be recorded throughout an entire year, on an hourly basis. On a heart monitor, heartbeat might be recorded over the period of a patient's stay in intensive care, say a week, and recordings might be taken every minute.

KEY POINT

A data logging system has the following characteristics:
- It involves a process monitored by instruments or sensors.
- The sensors are connected to an interface board which is in turn connected to the computer.
- The computer controlling the system samples the readings at regular time intervals.
- Readings are recorded, usually by storing them on backing store.
- Data is collected over a measured length of time, called the period of logging, and it is analysed. Analysis may take place while logging continues, or at the end of the period.
- Results may be displayed continuously:
  - in printed form, as numbers
  - as a screen display that updates continuously
  - as a graph that can be printed

The **time interval** and period of **logging** will vary according to the **type of data** being monitored.

Presentation of information, sharing and exchanging

OCR A OCR B
EDEXCEL
AQA A AQA B
WJEC
Key Skills ·

Data is **entered** into an **information system**, where it is **processed** and perhaps **stored** for a time.

It leaves the information system in the form of **output** when it is needed. It is now in the form of information that is useful in a particular context.

There are various ways of presenting **computer output**. When choosing the form that the information should take, it is important to think about the context, and the audience that will be receiving the **output information**. The number of the audience is important – one person, or a crowd – and other factors should be considered, for example:

- age of the audience
- familiarity of the audience with information systems and computers
- level of technical detail required by the audience
- any disabilities that audience members may have, for example, hearing or vision problems
- type of presentation required – mainly graphics, or text, or figures, or a mixture
- interests of the audience

Of course the type of output will also be governed by the output devices that are available. Information can be presented:

- as a screen display

You will need to think about the ways the output is to be used before stating an output method.

- as printout on paper (known as hard copy) – this could be pictures, graphs, charts or text
- with multimedia techniques – sound, pictures, graphs, charts, text
- as sound
- as virtual reality

Printed output

This is still the commonest way of **presenting information** from a computer system. Since most of the world was used to using paper, letters and books to pass information before computers were developed, the tendency has been to stick to using paper-based output methods because they are familiar. Things may change, however. Emails, although they take the form of **electronic letters**, are often never printed out on paper and the same applies to the millions of **web pages** that form the **World Wide Web**.

KEY POINT

> **Advantages/Disadvantages of printed paper output**
>
> Apart from force of habit, the advantages of using paper to present information are:
> - In the case of legal and other important documents, printed output provides visible proof of agreements or promises, or confirms what has been said at a meeting. If it is not printed, it is hard to prove that an email has been received and read.
> - Paper-based systems are available to most people and straightforward to use.
> - It is easier to read paper than a computer screen.
> - In the case of a long document or book, it is easier to flick backwards and forwards in a paper document than on screen.
> - Paper can be read on the move and in places where a computer might not be available.
>
> Disadvantages of using paper to present output are:
> - Paper is expensive to buy and bulky to store.
> - The use of paper is not environmentally friendly.
> - People photocopy paper-based output because they think they may lose it, so even more paper is used.
> - The pre-printing of many bills, invoices and other documents is expensive.
> - Moving paper around a commercial company takes time and organisation.

Screen output

Information normally appears as **output on the screen** of a PC before it is printed. In this case, the 'audience' is simply the user of the PC.

Graphics of all kinds are widely used in screen outputs because they make a visual impact when an audience sees them. Graphics can be presented on transparencies with overhead projectors, as series of slides produced by presentation software and displayed on a large screen by a projector, or as displays on normal computer screens.

Screen output on a larger scale is often used to sell products or services, or a company image to an audience, or to explain procedures and techniques for operating company systems or machinery.

Multimedia presentations are replacing less versatile screen presentations, particularly where the aim of the presentation is to show that a company is right up to date in the technology it offers.

Multimedia output

OCR A   OCR B
EDEXCEL
AQA A   AQA B
NICCEA
WJEC

 Images and events may be controlled via a mouse or keyboard.

A **multimedia presentation** involves a mixture of **text** and **graphics** with motion and sound, including **video**, **audio**, **animation** and **photographs**.

It is interactive, so that the audience can decide on different routes through the presentation.

Multimedia is ideal for learning new skills, as a **presentation** can be made to move along as fast as the learner wants, and will not be as impatient as a human teacher might be. **Multimedia** methods are now widely used in many learning contexts.

CDs are also more environmentally friendly than paper. Friends of the Earth estimate that a single CD-ROM full of text can save up to 15 trees' worth of paper.

> **KEY POINT**
> A multimedia presentation will require the necessary hardware and software – typically an ordinary PC with multimedia peripherals such as a CD and/or DVD drive, a sound card and speakers.

Multimedia presentations would not be possible without the technology of **CD-ROMs** and **DVDs**. These disks provide the **large storage capacity** needed for photographs, animation and video clips.

Sound output

Sound output often forms part of a **multimedia system**. Sound is very important where an audience has **vision problems**. It is used in games and in learning situations, where, for example, learners need to hear what words in another language sound like, or what kind of sound a certain animal makes. Music can be played too, for learning or enjoyment purposes.

Virtual reality

Virtual reality **presentations** are used for games and entertainment, but their use for more serious purposes is being developed all the time.

> **KEY POINT**
> In a military situation, for example, virtual reality can be used to create a fighting situation so that trainee soldiers can experience what a battle really feels like. Virtual reality may also be used in court to simulate road traffic accidents. The court and jury can experience exactly what a witness describes having seen.

PROGRESS CHECK

1. Briefly describe verification checks.
2. Briefly describe validation checks.
3. Why is it important that data should be accurate?
4. If information has been gained from a system, is the information necessarily true?
5. How does a basic data logging system work?
6. What sort of considerations might govern the choice of system output?
7. What are the main types of output from an information system?

1. They make sure that data entered into a system, or copied from another system, has been transmitted correctly. They are normally carried out by system users.
2. Software makes sure that data entered is sensible and will not cause problems in processing.
3. If inaccurate data is put into a system, inaccurate information will come out of the system. An information system cannot put right any data that is inaccurate.
4. There is no way of guaranteeing that information gained from an information system is true. There is no way of preventing people from publishing untrue information, and people may deliberately exploit this lack of control. The only guide is the reliability of the source of the information.
5. It automatically records data as it is produced. The data is collected by sensors or other instruments and the sensors are linked to a computer via an interface board. Readings are taken at regular time intervals, over a fixed period of time.
6. The type of audience will affect choice of output – age, technical ability, language ability, existence of any disabilities. Also the equipment available will govern choice. Some presentation equipment is very expensive, e.g. projectors, and might not be available.
7. The main types are screen displays, paper printouts (including pictures, graphs, charts and text), multimedia productions (including sound, pictures, graphs, charts and text), sound and virtual reality.

6.4 Misuse of data

LEARNING SUMMARY

After completing this section you should be able to:

- **describe two typical examples of misuse of data: electronic fraud and credit card fraud**
- **describe the provisions of the Computer Misuse Act, 1990**
- **describe the provisions of the Copyright, Designs and Patents Act, 1989**
- **describe the provisions of the Data Protection Act, 1998**

There are many opportunities for unscrupulous people and criminals to obtain data from **information systems** and use it for purposes that were not intended.

Information systems hold vast quantities of **personal information** about individuals, for example, that can be **accessed** by people who have the necessary skills, and misused.

A web site run by a recruitment agency would hold curricula vitae for the people who approached it to look for jobs. This **personal information** could be used to target people by a company looking for a market for a new range of products, or job-seekers could be contacted by people trying to discover damaging information about the companies the job-seekers are about to leave. These examples of misuse of data are not life-threatening, but the misuse of medical records held in a hospital, for example, could have life-threatening consequences.

Exam papers often contain questions about the laws surrounding the collection of personal information and why it should be kept secure.

Information systems also hold **vital data** about company operations. An unscrupulous operator might break into a company's system and cause havoc, for example, by altering salary rates for staff. This type of **misuse** might be simply malicious, or it could represent deliberate **electronic fraud**.

Electronic fraud

Careful staff recruitment can help prevent fraud, and some companies swap staff around different departments on a regular basis to avoid problems.

Electronic fraud is the use of communications systems to commit fraud for financial gain. (The word fraud means a criminal deception that is carried out with the intention of gaining an advantage.) A feature of this type of crime is that those who commit electronic fraud are normally very **technically competent** and able to take elaborate precautions against being caught. They are skilled at spotting weaknesses in systems, and exploiting them.

Electronic fraud may involve setting up false suppliers, who send invoices to a real company for payment. When payments are made to the suppliers by the unsuspecting company, the money is stolen. Great efforts are then made to make sure that the real company's accounting system will still balance so that the **fraud** is not noticed. Large companies try to guard against this type of fraud by making sure that several people are responsible for dealing with invoices so that making fraudulent payments would require the co-operation of several people.

Credit card fraud

You must understand the measures that can be taken to reduce fraud.

Credit card fraud involving stolen cards is a very common crime and costs credit card companies hundreds of millions of pounds each year.

A number of different ways of preventing this type of fraud have been developed:

- It is possible to authorise each transaction as it occurs by checking via a phone call or a special terminal that the card has not been stolen.
- It is also possible to make people key in their PIN at the checkout when making purchases using credit or payment cards. This method is widely used in European countries such as France.
- Biometric testing can be performed, where the user places an index finger into a machine that compares the fingerprint with one that has been recorded previously.
- The way a person writes their signature can also be checked, by concentrating on the timing, rhythm and pen movements.
- Some systems check the pattern on the retina of a person's eye.

Computer Misuse Act, 1990

You should understand the differences between hacking, fraud and viruses and measures to reduce the possibility of each affecting a system.

This Act was passed in order to deal with the relatively new crimes of **hacking**, **computer fraud** and **computer viruses** (see also pages 123 and 125). Before this law, for example, a hacker could only be prosecuted for the theft of electricity.

The following offences can now be dealt with:

- **Hacking** – unauthorised access to any program or data held in a computer. The penalty is a maximum fine of £2,000 and a six-month prison sentence.
- **Computer fraud and blackmail**. The penalty is an unlimited fine and a maximum five-year prison sentence.
- **Viruses** – unauthorised modification of the contents of a computer that might damage the operation of programs and/or affect the reliability of data. The penalty is an unlimited fine and maximum five-year prison sentence.

The Copyright, Designs and Patents Act, 1989

This Act makes the copying of computer software, or software piracy, a criminal offence. The Act covers the following activities:

- stealing software
- using illegally copied software and manuals
- running purchased software on two or more machines at the same time, without an appropriate licence bought from the software supplier

Legal penalties for breaking this law include unlimited fines, and up to two years in prison.

Researchers estimate that at least half of the software used has been **copied illegally**. In some countries, **pirated** software accounts for 90% of the total.

The following two organisations attempt to curb illegal copying:

- FAST (Federation Against Software Theft) founded in 1984. This is a non-profit making organisation that promotes legal use of software.
- BSA (Business Software Alliance) tries to make businesses and their employees aware of the law and to encourage its implementation.

Data Protection Act, 1998

The rapid growth in the power and coverage of **information systems** means that **databases** are able to hold huge quantities of data which can be distributed around the world in seconds.

Much of this data relates to individual people, and may be of a **personal nature**. However, we all expect to have a **right to privacy**. We do not expect to have personal details such as our age, personal family details, medical records, financial data and our political or religious beliefs to be freely available to anyone.

The Data Protection Act was introduced to control the technological ability to transmit data and to protect people's right to privacy.

Any **person**, **organisation** or **company** wishing to hold personal information about people must register with the Office of the **Data Protection Commissioner**.

> The first Act became law in 1984 but was replaced in 1998 by a new Act that included the Directive of the European Commission. The new Act also covered manual records, as well as those held on computers.

KEY POINT

The basic principles of the Data Protection Act, 1998, are given here. Personal data must:
- be processed fairly and lawfully (this principle contains the most details in the Act because, for the other principles, different conditions apply according to the type of data held)
- be obtained for specified and lawful purposes
- be adequate, relevant and not excessive for the purpose
- be accurate and up-to-date
- not be kept any longer than necessary
- be processed within the rights of data subjects
- be kept secure against loss, damage and unauthorised and unlawful processing
- not be transferred to countries outside the European Economic Area

For the purpose of data protection, it is important to be clear about what 'personal data' means. The term is defined as:

Data that can identify a living person, and allow an opinion to be expressed about that person.

Data about an individual can be further **classified** as '**sensitive**' personal data and the use of this type of data is more restricted. 'Sensitive' personal data includes details of:

- racial or ethnic origins
- religious beliefs
- political opinions
- membership of trades unions
- state of physical or mental health
- sexual life

The sixth basic principle of the Act refers to the **rights of data subjects**. A data subject is a person on whom data is held. The 1998 Act increased the rights of data subjects considerably.

A summary of these rights follows:

The individual can:

- ask for and be given a copy of data held
- prevent processing of data if it is likely to cause damage or distress
- prevent data being used for direct marketing
- prevent automated decisions being made on the basis of data held
- receive compensation for damage and distress caused by use of data
- have data corrected, blocked or erased if it is inaccurate
- make a request to the Data Protection Commissioner if he or she believes that the Act has been contravened

KEY POINT

The 1998 Act allows for exemptions to its provisions to be made under the following conditions:
- where national security is concerned
- where crime or taxation are concerned
- where data relates to health, education and social work
- where data is used in regulatory activities by 'watch dog' organisations
- where data is being used for research, history and statistics
- where data is required by law and in connection with legal proceedings being disclosed
- where data is held for domestic purposes, for example, for household, personal or family use

PROGRESS CHECK

1. What are the basic provisions of the Computer Misuse Act, 1990?
2. What are the basic provisions of the Copyright, Designs and Patents Act, 1989?

1. The Act was introduced to create penalties for the 'new' crimes of hacking, computer fraud and planting viruses in information systems.
2. The Act was introduced to create penalties for the 'new' crime of computer piracy. It covers the offences of stealing software, using illegally copied software and manuals, and running purchased software on multiple machines, without an appropriate licence bought from the software supplier.

Sample GCSE questions

1 State three criminal offences that occur due to misuse of the Internet.
State three social or moral offences that occur due to misuse of the Internet.

Try to think of both moral and legal points and put them in the right place.

Example answer:
One   *legal problems*
Two   *copying people's work - plagiarism*
Three *fraud*

One   *social and moral problems: selling lists of names leading to junk mail*
Two   *pornography on the Internet*
Three *spreading viruses*   **[6]**

2 A school secretary types data into a database.

Think about ways data can be checked both electronically and manually.

(a) State two ways that the data could be verified manually.
One   *visually*
Two   *through double entry (both being types of verification check)*   **[2]**

(b) State whether checking can be verified automatically.

Yes, by running verification checks such as parity checks, and validation checks such as type checks and presence checks.   **[2]**

3 Two types of validation techniques are range checks and length checks. Explain the difference between these two types of check.

A range check verifies whether data is within approved limits and a length check checks verifies that data is exactly equal to a pre-determined length of character strings.   **[2]**

4 Give two software methods of preventing illegal access to computer records.

Encryption or use of passwords.   **[2]**

5 Describe four ways the Data Protection Act 1998 aims to protect individuals from the misuse of personal data.

Questions on the Data Protection Act are often on exam papers. Try to remember the key points in the Act.

Example answer:

Data users must register; data must be obtained lawfully; consent of data subject must be sought; data must be obtained fairly; data must be up to date; data can only be used for the specified purpose; data must be accurate; data must not be kept longer than necessary; individual is entitled to have access to data on him or herself.   **[4]**

Exam practice questions

1 Briefly describe two typical examples of misuse of data.

....

....

....

....

.... **[4]**

2 What are the basic provisions of the Data Protection Act, 1998?

....

....

....

....

.... **[6]**

3 A school database contains personal information; all personal information held by organisations should be:

1. kept confidential ☐
2. held only as printed records ☐
3. checked for viruses ☐
4. corrected using a spell checker ☐ **[1]**

4 Passwords are often used to protect

1. systems from virus infection ☐
2. disks and files from data corruption ☐
3. users from dangerous environments ☐
4. confidential information from unauthorised access ☐ **[1]**

5 The school secretary enters new pupil records and changes other information on the school database. What check should be made by the secretary before saving and printing out copies?

1. data-type check ☐
2. grammar check ☐
3. proof-read check ☐
4. spell check ☐ **[1]**

6 To prevent unauthorised use of the database, access should be controlled by use of a:

1. virus ☐
2. password ☐
3. CD-ROM ☐
4. directory ☐ **[1]**

7.1 ICT in commerce and at work

LEARNING SUMMARY

After completing this section you will be able to:

- **explore the impact of ICT in a commercial context**
- **describe the impact of ICT in terms of jobs and the way people work**

> **Some exam papers (e.g. OCR syllabus B (Full Course Paper)) are entirely based on the application of ICT knowledge in context. This means a real commercial company will be used for all of the exam questions.**

Most commercial operations now employ **information systems**. We have computer systems in our homes, schools, colleges, and in any other place where there is a need to process data and transmit the information gained between **human users**. We take it for granted that it is possible to send **electronic communications** to the other side of the world in a matter of minutes, or to process quantities of **data** received from **remote** sources to obtain results from a **centrally located** unit.

The first electronic computers were constructed around 50 years ago and used glass tubes called **valves**. These first computers were used to **calculate** firing tables for field guns and to crack German codes during the Second World War. Their processing power was tiny by today's standards, and the machines were very large and consumed enormous volumes of power. The use of smaller, **less energy** expensive computers in businesses, homes and schools began to be widespread only about 20 years ago.

Computer use is growing all the time. Computers become smaller but more **sophisticated**; they have larger **memories**, better **displays**, faster **processing** and new **features**, but their price remains fairly stable, or even drops in some cases.

Examination questions often focus upon how ICT has changed our lives.

Computer use now affects our daily lives in many ways, some more obvious than others. For example, the millions of telephone calls made every day could not be handled without computers, nor could the millions of **debit** and **credit** card payments that we make.

The entire **economy** of a country such as the United Kingdom is governed by the use of computers and, without them, **standards of living** would fall. It would not be possible for supermarkets to keep their shelves well **stocked** with fresh food without computers. Some people say they would like to go back to old-fashioned methods, but this would be likely to cause price rises and all kinds of supply difficulties.

Exam questions often ask you to contrast methods of working with and without ICT.

Email communication and access to information via the **World Wide Web** is having a great effect on our lives. It is enabling more and more people to work from home, and still keep in visual contact with other colleagues via **cameras** mounted on **computer monitors**. The traditional office to which people travel every weekday may soon be a thing of the past.

KEY POINT

Some people have thought that the introduction of computers in working situations would lead to a great reduction in the use of paper. In fact, the reverse is true as computers can generate far more paper-based documents than we had before. Quantities of computerised mail delivered to our homes (bills, forms, advertising leaflets) show that a lot of information about people is held on computer files. Some of the data held is of a highly confidential nature, and some of it may be incorrect if errors have been made in data sourcing and entry. The misuse of data held about us could have a serious effect on our lives.

The introduction of **computers** has resulted in the loss of many jobs. At first, many of the jobs lost were those of **unskilled** workers employed on **repetitive** tasks that were replaced by machines. More recently, computerisation has replaced jobs across many working areas. **Specialist computer programs** can replace middle managers who used to make

Robotic car sprayer

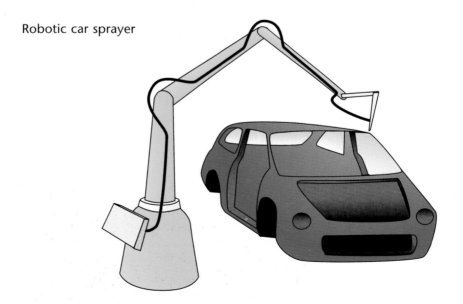

complex decisions for companies using tried and tested **procedures**. Software can make the same decisions more cheaply.

If you are asked how ICT has changed working practices, remember to give a balanced view with both positive and negative points.

KEY POINT

A dilemma is faced by many employers, trades unions and the government, related to investment in computerised systems in manufacturing. Where a manufacturing organisation invests in computerised systems, it will become more competitive as productivity rises and labour costs are reduced. However, some of its workers may lose their jobs and this has a cost also. If it does not computerise, high labour costs and lower productivity make its goods less competitive, so that the company loses its market share, profits drop, and all the workers may eventually lose their jobs. In addition, the manufacturer loses the ability to manufacture goods at a standard comparable to more technologically advanced producers. If this happens on a country-wide scale, a whole nation's economy can be affected. It is unlikely that a government would wish to see this happen.

The growth of computer use has led to an increase in the number of jobs in certain sectors, however. While jobs have been lost in **manufacturing**, the number of jobs in **service industries** such as shops, hotels, leisure and catering has increased. This is partly due to an increase in wealth generated by the more **technologically advanced** industries. Also, ways of working are changing.

The **call centre**, for example, where many operators sit at **computer terminals** and answer customer queries on incoming phone lines, did not exist before the widespread introduction of computers. Many new jobs that are directly related to ICT and computing have also been created. **Computer specialists** are required in both manufacturing and service industries.

Many people have had to **retrain** in new areas of work as **computerised systems** have replaced **traditional** ways of working. Before the introduction of computers on a large scale, it was normal to expect to train for a job and to stay in a similar sort of job throughout your working life. The emphasis today is on **flexibility**. People have to accept that they may need to learn new skills on a regular basis to keep up with the pace of change in the working environment. It is also important that people understand how computers and information systems work, and the effect that ICT has on their lives so that they can have an opinion about changes that are taking place. Ideally, they should be in a position to influence change and aim for a better quality of life.

PROGRESS CHECK

1. What has led to computers becoming both smaller and more sophisticated?
2. Name two areas where computers affect our daily lives.
3. Has the introduction of ICT reduced the use of paper?
4. How are email communications affecting the way we work?
5. What type of jobs have been replaced by ICT?

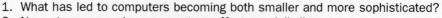

5. Middle management jobs, unskilled jobs and repetitive tasks.
4. Enabling more people to work from home.
3. No.
2. Telephone calls; debit and credit card payments.
1. Larger memories; better displays; faster processing; smaller processors.

7.2 Mail-order company

After completing this section, you should be able to:

- describe in detail how information systems are used in the context of a mail-order company
- explain the different types of report that can be generated by computer systems

A context where information systems are vital is that of mail-order businesses. Mail-order is becoming more and more popular as a method of shopping.

Costins

Soft pinks for that summer barbeque. Another dream kitchen offer

Step into Summer

Some examinations focus upon a specific area of study. The same considerations relating to staff skills and changing jobs apply across contexts.

Organisation of mail-order companies

OCR A
EDEXCEL
AQA A · AQA B
WJEC

Traditionally, mail-order was based upon large catalogues delivered to the homes of those who wished to buy. Paper catalogues are still used, but there is enormous growth in mail-order through dedicated television channels, and through shopping sites on the World Wide Web.

Information systems form the foundation of modern mail-order business, providing basic stock level information and keeping track of individual **customer accounts**, returned goods and payment for items that are delivered on a cash-on-delivery basis.

KEY POINT

A typical mail-order business will have a network of personal computers with terminals **in the** accounts department, sales department, technical department **and** warehouse. **It will keep separate files for stock, orders, returns and accounts, but these are likely to be tables within a** relational database **so that there are links between the files.**

A relational database is made up of rows and columns. For example:

Name	Town	County
Downing, D.	Chester	Cheshire
Covington, M.	Lincoln	Lincolnshire

The table defines a relation between the things in each row. It says that Chester is the town for D. Downing, and that Cheshire is the county for Chester, and so on. An important operation of a relational database is that it can join two or more tables, which means cross-referencing information between them. For example, the names in the table above could be cross-referenced to another table containing information on purchases and orders. (A database with only one table is called a **flat file database**.)

To examine how one part of the mail-order information system works, we can look at the section that deals with returns.

A large mail-order business is likely to have a large number of goods that are returned and it will make its returns policy clear to its customers. Customers may want to **return goods** either because they do not like them, or because they do not fit, or because they are faulty or not what the customer expected. All returned items must be **booked into the system** and it will be important to check that items bought elsewhere are not sent in, and that customers return any **rejected** goods quickly, and not after they have used them for some time. To check these points, the returns system will look up the record in the **order file**, using the **order number**, to find out when the order was placed.

Try to represent your thinking using charts and diagrams.

- If an item can be accepted, a **record** is created in the **returns file**.
- If an item is returned because it is unsuitable or does not fit, its condition will be checked to make sure it is not damaged or worn.
- If the item has been returned as faulty, it will be checked over by a technician to establish whether it is really faulty or whether perhaps the customer just did not know how to use or connect up the item.

Many mail-order companies would not want to accept returns of goods that are not faulty. When the technician tests an item in detail, he or she will enter the results of the test and his or her identification number into the record for the item. Depending on company policy, if the item does work, it may be sent back to the customer and the record in the return file will show that this has happened.

Any item that does prove to be faulty will be returned to the original supplier and the customer will receive a new one as a **replacement**. Each new step will be recorded on the system so that a record is kept of how many items of each kind have to be returned. The mail-order company will not want to pay for faulty items from the supplier.

The returns system will be able to produce a number of different reports. Three examples of typical reports are given below:

For example, the system can list all the details of items that have been returned, and which have been found to be faulty.

Returned Item Report					
Date: 28/07/2001					
Supplier	Product	Total produced	Returned by customer	Found to be faulty	%
230098	W345	8455	12	8	0.09
789000	B567	12996	4	4	0.03
100987	M678	23	2	1	4.3
325667	R567	987654	230	130	0.013
678999	U899	3456	12	10	0.28
876540	W346	134	25	8	5.9

The database calculates the number of faulty items as a percentage of total sales of that item and this report will show the buying department which items are proving to be unreliable. If one particular supplier seems to produce numbers of faulty items, the mail-order company is likely to stop using that supplier and it will discontinue the item if another supplier cannot be found.

The system will be able to report on staff performance also.

Staff Performance Report					
Date: 28/07/2001					
Staff number	Job	Total orders checked	Returns due to faults	Hours worked	% Error
S123	Checker	84559	38	36	0.04
S556	Checker	12996	48	36	0.37
S557	Checker	23886	29	28	0.12
S445	Checker	98765	23	42	0.02
S988	Checker	3456	92	24	2.7
S999	Checker	1340	25	23	1.9

It can show details of each technician's work, including how many items have been tested, and how often the result has been wrong. An incompetent technician can be expensive to a company because customers will be angry if they are told that goods work properly when they do not. Also, suppliers of components normally charge for checking goods that are returned as faulty, but are really in working order.

Some customers may return many of the goods they order with a variety of excuses.

Customer Returns Report					
Date: 28/07/2001					
Customer number	Name	Total orders	Returned items	Faulty	Not faulty
CU456	Rogers	456	3	2	1
CU789	Patel	9887	4	4	0
CU56	Morrison	123	2	1	1
CU007	Cushing	56788	23	13	10
CU789	Smith	3456	12	1	11
CU444	Wang	334	25	8	17

The system can produce a report that will list customers who do this. Although a mail-order company may not be able to do much about a private customer who repeatedly returns goods, a trade customer who buys and returns on a large scale may be charged for excessive returns.

Security

OCR A
EDEXCEL
AQA A   AQA B
WJEC

An information system used by a mail-order company requires tight **security**. A lot of the data held is **confidential** and all of it is of value to the business of the company.

KEY POINT

Users will be limited as to the reports that they can access. For example, the technician staff performance report is likely to be accessible only to the returns department manager. Individual technicians will be able to enter data about results of tests into the system, but they will not be able to add records to the file, nor to delete whole records. They will not be able to edit fields that describe the item, nor to alter customer and supplier data.

The subjects described in other chapters of this book are now being applied to a context. You will need to draw upon your knowledge and apply it to the set business.

Only the staff who receive returned items will be able to actually create a **returns record**. To do this, they will need a valid order number and an **item code** from the order record. Returns staff will not be able to create **new customer records**. This will be done in the sales department.

The aim of the returns system will be to process returns efficiently so that cost is minimised and customers remain satisfied. Persistently faulty items can be identified and removed from the range, and difficult customers can also be listed. Staff performance can be monitored so that outstandingly good staff can be rewarded. Also, the returns system will function as part of the whole information system of the mail-order company to ensure that it operates as economically as possible.

PROGRESS CHECK

1. What new jobs have been created as a result of ICT?
2. What type of database does a mail-order company use?
3. Give three types of report that can be generated by a mail-order computer system.

3. A returned items report, staff performance report, customer returns report.
2. A relational database.
1. Call centre jobs, computer specialists.

Sample GCSE questions

1 Why is security important to a mail-order company?

*A lot of data will be confidential and valuable to the
business of the company.* **[2]**

2 How would a mail-order company ensure security within the
company?

*By restricting access to individuals within the company;
by using passwords.* **[2]**

3 Describe why the accurate recording of returns is important to a
mail order company.

*A large mail-order business is likely to have a large number of
goods that are returned. Customers may want to return
goods either because they do not like them, or because
they do not fit, or because they are faulty or not what
the customer expected. All returned items must be booked
into the system and it will be important to check that items
bought elsewhere are not sent in, and that customers
return any rejected goods quickly, and not after they have
used them for some time.* **[6]**

> *This type of question is often hard to revise for as you do not know in advance what organisation the questions will be based upon. Some GCSEs do give you advance warning about the context the questions will be based upon. If they do, make sure that you understand the needs of the organisation before you sit the exam paper. If they do not, you will need to apply your general knowledge of ICT to the set context.*

Exam practice questions

1   State two advantages and two disadvantages of the introduction of ICT.

....

....

....

....

....   **[4]**

2   Where has the number of jobs increased as a result of ICT?

....

....

....

....

....   **[3]**

3   In which departments are information systems used in a modern mail-order business?

....

....

....

....

....   **[3]**

4   What are the two main areas in which ICT is used in a mail-order business?

....

....

....

....

....   **[3]**

8.1 Health and safety

LEARNING SUMMARY

After completing this section, you should be able to:

● *describe typical health problems that may result from prolonged use of computers*
● *discuss the risks of using mobile telephones and in-car communications systems*
● *explain the legal obligations of employers with regard to their employees using computer systems*
● *suggest recommendations for the best design of work areas using computer systems*

Working safely

OCR A   OCR B
EDEXCEL
AQA A   AQA B

The ICT working environment is relatively safe. However users must avoid:

● bad posture and physical stress
● eye strain
● hazards resulting from equipment or workplace layout

A comfortable working position is important to avoid physical stress, eye strain and safety hazards. This may be achieved through:

● comfortable seating
● suitable desk and VDU position
● suitable keyboard position
● brief rest periods
● avoiding long periods of continuous VDU work
● surrounding area that includes near and distant objects upon which the eyes may focus
● layout of cables and equipment (to avoid tripping)
● insulation of cables (from electrical supplies)

When setting up or using ICT systems, users must be able to work safely. To do this they must ensure that:

- cables do not cause an obstacle hazard
- cables and connectors are electrically safe
- consumables are replaced correctly
- physical working environment and position (ergonomics) is acceptable

The following health problems have been identified as having a link to **prolonged** use of computers in **traditional** office settings:

- repetitive strain injury (RSI)
- headache
- backache
- skin rashes
- eye strain

Health and Safety issues are becoming more important in exploring ICT use. These issues are important when designing systems and as a disadvantage in the use of ICT.

KEY POINT

There are various commonsense measures that you can take to avoid such problems. Points to look at are:
- angle, brightness and contrast of the monitor
- position of any text you wish to copy from
- type of chair you sit on – it should have an adjustable back rest (both angle and height) and adjustable seat height. It should also be on castors. The chair may also need to be on a mat if the floor is slippery
- position of the keyboard and mouse on the desk
- position of a footrest under the desk
- how long you spend in front of the computer without a break

Repetitive Strain Injury (RSI)

OCR A   OCR B
EDEXCEL
AQA A   AQA B

RSI is caused by the joints in the fingers and lower arms being constantly pounded by **typing at high speed**. It causes pain in the joints and can cause long-term disability if nothing is done about it.

Exam questions sometimes ask you to identify problems associated with computer use. At other times they will ask how to avoid set problems.

KEY POINT

To guard against RSI:
- use a keyboard with good ergonomic design
- have the keyboard positioned correctly
- make sure your typing technique is good
- take regular breaks
- you can also buy wrist guards which ease fatigue when you are using the keyboard for long periods

Eye strain

OCR A   OCR B
EDEXCEL
AQA A   AQA B

Eye strain is quite common in many types of close work. A recent study of **Display Screen** operators indicated that nearly 70% of them suffered some sort of eye problem ranging from eye strain or irritated eyes to blurred vision. The use of a screen glare deflector can help some users, and it is always a good idea to look away from a screen and at a distant object at fairly frequent intervals. This makes the eyes adjust their focus and exercises the muscles involved.

KEY POINT   **Regular computer users should always have regular eye checks.**

Computer use and reproduction

There have been some reports that women who have used display screens for long periods have produced abnormal births. This is connected to the radiation given out by display screens when they are working. (Many other electrical appliances also give out **radiation**.) Most of the **radiation** emanates from the back and sides of a display screen. At present, after a great deal of research, there is little evidence that display screens do any damage.

Mobile phones and in-car communications systems

The radiation given off by mobile phones is also believed to be capable of causing brain tumours. A lot of research continues to be carried out into this potential danger.

Increasingly often, **mobile phones** form part of **information systems**. The frequent use of these phones is also associated with certain health risks. They are believed to cause neck strain and headaches.

Many drivers also unwisely use mobile phones while they are driving. This distracts them from watching the road, and may contribute to causing accidents. A recent study carried out by the University of Toronto indicated that a driver using a mobile phone while on the move was four times more likely to be involved in a collision, and six times more likely during the first few minutes of a conversation.

Other components of communications systems now being introduced into cars are also giving rise to extensive research about risks of distracting drivers. Examples are **navigation systems**, and **vehicle monitoring and maintenance systems**, where directions or information about the state of the vehicle can be displayed on a screen.

The ability of **WAP** mobile phones to send and receive emails and access web sites could also lead to driver distraction.

Recent recommendations suggested that it was better to use a **headset** with a mobile phone, but then another report stated that headsets were even more dangerous than the phones themselves, as they pick up **radiation** from other **appliances** also. It is sensible to try to limit the use of a mobile phone to a reasonable level.

Protection of the workforce

A law now requires employers to provide the following, in an attempt to avoid health problems related to use of computer systems:

- **Inspections**. Desks, chairs, computers and other equipment should be inspected to make sure that they meet the required standard.

- **Training**. Employees should have training on health and safety matters.

- **Job design**. A job should be designed so that anyone regularly using computers has periodic breaks or changes in activity.

- **Eye tests**. The employer should arrange for regular free eye tests, with any necessary glasses provided at the employer's expense, for all employees regularly using computers.

Minimum requirements for computer systems and furniture have also been set. All new furniture and equipment bought must meet these standards:

- **Display screens**. These must have a stable picture, with no flicker. There must be no reflection off the screen. Brightness, contrast, angle and swivel must be easily adjustable.

- **Keyboards**. Keyboards must be separate from screens and capable of being tilted. Keyboards should be easy to use and the surface should be matt to avoid glare. There must be enough space for people to be able to change position.

- **Desks**. Desks must be large enough to take the computer, any necessary peripherals, and paperwork. They should not reflect too much light. Where a lot of data is input from paper copy, an adjustable document holder should be provided to avoid uncomfortable head movements.

- **Chairs**. Chairs must be adjustable and comfortable, allowing easy freedom of movement. A foot rest must be available on request.

- **Lighting**. There must be no glare or reflection on computer screens. Windows must have adjustable coverings.

- **Noise**. Noise should not be loud enough to distract attention and disturb speech.

- **Software**. Software must be easy to use and appropriate to the user's needs and experience.

- **Other matters**. Emissions of heat, humidity and radiation must be kept at adequate levels.

When designing an office or working area for computer systems, it is useful to consider the following points:

- Single pendant lamps (as in most houses) produce **glare** on a screen. It is better to use fluorescent tubes with plastic covers that **diffuse glare** and spread out the light.

- Carpets made of artificial fibres should be avoided because they cause **static electricity** which can **destroy data** held on **magnetic disks**. It is better to use floor coverings made from natural fibres.

- Windows should have adjustable blinds that can be closed or partially closed to prevent the sun from creating glare on **screens**.

- If it is not possible for them to be fitted under the floor, cables should be carefully positioned so that people will not trip over them.

- The room should have plenty of power sockets. **Overloading** a small number of sockets can be dangerous.

PROGRESS CHECK

1. What health problems may result from prolonged use of computers in office-type settings?
2. Why are carpets made from artificial fibre problematic in an ICT enviroment?
3. What precautions should regular users of computers take to protect their eyesight?

1. Health problems most commonly linked with computer use are repetitive strain injury (RSI) which affects hands and lower arms, backache, eye strain, headaches and skin rashes.
2. They cause static electricity which can destroy data held on magnetic disks.
3. Regular computer users should always have regular eye checks.

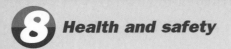

Sample GCSE questions

1   An office secretary works at a computer all day. There are a number of known medical problems that can arise through continuous use of computers.

State two pieces of advice that you would give to the secretary and give a reason for each.

Example answers:
One   *take frequent breaks - to avoid eye strain and risk of headache.*
Two   *use a correct chair - to avoid back problems.*   **[4]**

2   A large office contains a local area network. Six people work in the office and a number of other people pass through the office during the working day.

Describe four precautions that should be taken to ensure that the office is safe to use.

Example answers:
One   *position of monitors* ◄
Two   *computers fixed down*
Three *position of desks/work benches*
Four   *position of cables connecting the network*   **[8]**

> *Try to think of different precautions. You will not gain marks for the same point written down using different words.*

3   A school needs to convert one classroom into a research area where pupils will be able to access information on CDs and the Internet. The room will contain 15 computers. Suggest four factors that should be taken into account when choosing a suitable classroom. ◄

Example answers:
One   *size of room.*
Two   *location of room.*
Three *electricity supply to the room.*
Four   *number of power points available.*   **[8]**

> *You should be able to answer this type of question by thinking of your own school system.*

Exam practice questions

1   Describe the risks associated with the use of mobile telephones and in-car
    communications systems.

    ....

    ....

    ....

    ....

    ....   **[6]**

2   Describe how employers are obliged to look after their employees who use computer
    systems.

    ....

    ....

    ....

    ....

    ....   **[4]**

3   List important points to bear in mind when fitting out a work area where computers will be
    used.

    ....

    ....

    ....

    ....   **[3]**

Exam practice answers

Chapter 1 Information systems

1 The system processes the raw data into useful information and outputs it as a visible or audible result of data processing. Some outputs feed back into the system to control future outputs.

2 A signal is digital if data in it is represented as electrical 'on' and 'off' signals that correspond to binary digits. The data is therefore represented as a succession of 1s and 0s. Analogue signals are represented as signals that vary within a predefined range.

Chapter 2 Hardware

1 A standard computer is usually found on a desk in an office or work place and is likely to be used for tasks such as word processing, account management or production of graphics. Small, programmable devices that are called computers are fitted inside cars and can control the operation of the car, as well as carrying out other tasks such as direction finding. PDAs are hand-held devices that can be used to help keep track of a busy working and social life. They offer functions such as: keeping track of appointments and regular commitments; storing the names and addresses of contacts and friends; downloading email from a personal computer so that it can be read offline on the PDA; offering a full range of calculating facilities; preparing, editing, sending and receiving faxes.

Mobile telephones and the latest televisions can also form part of information systems. Mobile telephones with WAP technology can access the Internet and send and receive emails, and televisions can offer processing functions and interaction with users.

2 The advantages of digital cameras are that they do not need film and there are no expensive developing costs. Any unwanted images can be deleted immediately and images that are required can be put into a document without the need for a scanner. Images can be sent to other people via the Internet, and can be edited without the need for professional darkroom work. Specialised software such as PhotoShop allows users to remove unwanted details in photographs, add extra features and adjust colour and contrast. However, the disadvantages are that digital cameras are expensive and unless high quality photographic paper is used to print pictures, quality is not as good as that produced by printing traditional film.

3 Inputting data by speech recognition means that the operator does not need to be able to use his or her hands. The main disadvantage is that the software has to be trained to recognise the speech pattern of each individual user. It works best with a special microphone positioned just centimetres below the mouth, as this avoids picking up surrounding noise or breathing sounds. The software must also be trained to recognise specialist or technical words that may not feature in a normal vocabulary. Users of speech recognition may also have to be trained as many people find it difficult to speak in a 'writing' style.

4 ROM and RAM are the two types of main store memory located in the central processing unit of a computer. They are instantly accessible, and data held in ROM and RAM can be read at high speed. No mechanical movement is required for data transfer.

Read Only Memory, ROM, is held on a chip inside the processor and is used to hold data that cannot be changed by the user. Programs that control the operating system are stored on ROM chips when a computer is manufactured. ROM is non-volatile memory.

Random Access Memory, RAM, is held on a chip, but only temporarily. It is volatile memory. RAM is used to hold both data and programs during processing. It also holds the contents of the screen during use.

5 Hard disks are fixed inside the hard disk drive of a computer and are used to store the operating system, applications software and user's files for a PC; store the operating system, software and files for a local area network (LAN); store work awaiting printing.

Floppy disks are used to hold applications packages supplied to users, to hold data files, and to store back-ups of working files.

CD-ROMs offer more storage space than floppy disks. They are used to hold applications packages, graphics, encyclopaedias, photographs and reference materials of all kinds. CD-Rs are useful for storing back-ups of large files.

Magnetic tape used to be widely used for back-ups of company files. It is still used in some companies to hold data such as payrolls that have to be processed for all employees on the same date.

DVDs offer even more storage capacity than CDs. They are used for applications packages, multimedia programs and full-length films.

6 Disadvantages are that it is not suitable for use in noisy environments, nor in very quiet environments

where other people are working. No permanent copy is produced and messages are not always clear. If a message is not understood the first time, the computer can only repeat it in exactly the same way, so that it may not be understood the second time either.

Chapter 3 *Software*

1 **(a)** 2; **(b)** 2; **(c)** 1; **(d)** 1; **(e)** 2.

2 **(a)** 1; **(b)** 4; **(c)** 3; **(d)** 3; **(e)** 2; **(f)** 1; **(g)** 3; **(h)** 1.

3 **(a)** 4; **(b)** 1; **(c)** 2; **(d)** 1; **(e)** 2; **(f)** 2; **(g)** 3.

4 A command-driven interface requires the user to enter a precise command into the system to get something done. The command is normally entered via a keyboard. This type of interface has largely been replaced by the other two types.

With a menu-driven interface, system functions are accessed through lists of commands or options that appear on the screen. A mouse or touch sensitive pad, or keyboard, are used to make a selection.

A graphical user interface offers the user an extensive range of pictures, or icons, from which to make selections using a mouse, touch sensitive pad, or keyboard. The icons are designed to be self-explanatory. Pull-down menus are also a feature of a graphical user interface.

5 It allocates memory for storing programs and data so that when data is needed, it can be found easily. The system takes care of data storage in the computer system's memory. It must keep track of what space is available as well as what has already been allocated.

It has routines for handling input and output operations. It accepts commands and data from the user via input devices, interprets commands, transfers data to memory, retrieves data from memory and sends it to output devices. It is able to tell the difference between the different peripherals so that data is not mis-routed.

It looks after transfers of data between the backing store and memory, both where data is being read from disk, and transferred to disk.

The operating system also manages system security. Many systems allocate certain rights to particular users who are allocated unique passwords.

6 Low-level programming languages are closer to machine code, the only language directly understood by the computer. High-level languages are more elaborate and are used for sophisticated programming.

Assembly language is a low-level language. It uses simple commands and is easier for a programmer to use than machine code. Examples of high-level languages are

C++ – used for graphics and for development of commercial software.

HTML – used to create websites.

JAVA – used to write software that will search for things on the Internet.

LOGO – used to teach children about programming and using computers.

7 Machine code is the most basic programming language. It is the only language that can be understood by a computer and so all program commands must be converted into machine code (or language) before the computer can actually decipher them. This code is binary, consisting of 1s and 0s, and is often machine specific. Commands written in machine code produce rapid results because they do not have to be translated into another language and, for this reason, many games and simulation programs are written in machine code.

8 You should first scan the documentation supplied with the software to see if it can be used to produce the outcome that you hope for, and if it appears easy to use.

Then try out a test run on the software to see if it performs as it claims to do, and to see if it is user friendly. The methods of input and output should suit what you want to do and the type of data you have. If the program is interactive, observe whether the type of user interface is suitable. Find out if the program is versatile, adaptable, robust and reliable.

Chapter 4 *Networks and the Internet*

1 A Local Area Network is a network that is confined to a small area, usually within a single building.

Advantages of using a local area network are that:

- Costly resources such as printers can be shared by all computers.
- Central backing store can be provided in one so all work is saved together.
- Software can be shared, and upgrading is easier too.
- Central back-up can take place automatically at regular intervals.
- Data can be shared across the network. This would allow several people to work on the same project.
- If the data being shared is in a database, several people will be able to use the database at the same time, but they will not be able to edit the same record at the same time. This avoids the confusion that would result if several people were trying to edit data at the same time.
- Local email messages can be sent to people working at other terminals on the network. This can save time and ensures that messages get to the right place.
- There may be a local Intranet. This works like the World Wide Web, with pages of information, but use of it is free within a LAN.

Disadvantages of using a Local Area Network are that:

- The use of email within the network can lead to workers wasting time sending messages that do not relate to work.

- Long print queues may develop where only one or two printers serve many terminals.

- Network security can be a problem. If a virus gets into one computer, it is likely to spread quickly across the network because it will get into the central backing store.

- Users of the network have to have user names and passwords. Some users are not very good at keeping passwords secret, or they may use passwords that are easy to guess. Other people can then log on to the network.

- If the dedicated file server fails, work stored on shared hard disk drives will not be accessible and it will not be possible to use network printers either.

- Cabling can be expensive, and in a busy office situation, cabling must often be placed under the floor so that people will not trip over it. If connecting cables are damaged, some sections of the network can become isolated.

2   The ways of setting out a network are called topologies. The four ways are:

Ring topology – In a ring topology, all of the terminals or other nodes in the network are connected together in a circle, with no device having any more importance than any other.

Line (bus) topology – In this layout, data is sent to all nodes on the network at the same time. Devices are positioned along a line, rather like bus stops.

Star topology – In this type of network, a central controller forms the principal node, while the subsidiary nodes form the points of the star.

Hierarchical network – In a hierarchical network, one or more computers is more powerful than the rest. The more powerful server, (or servers), looks after printing, file maintenance and other peripherals. Less powerful computers called clients are connected to the network. The clients may have no disk drives nor processing power of their own. They make use of the functions provided by the server.

3   Software called a web browser is needed to make use of the features of the World Wide Web.

The WWW is divided into millions of sites called websites. If you know the Uniform Resource Locator of the site you are looking for, you can type this straight into the address prompt of the browser. The address takes a standard format, and the full form of the address will start http://www......... Many browsers will accept a URL without the http:// part of it. If you do not know the URL of a site, or you want to locate information about a particular topic, you use software known as a search engine to help track down the information. The search engine can sift through large quantities of text and other data, according to specific instructions that it has been given.

If you want to visit certain sites regularly, the browser can bookmark the URLs of these sites so that they can be accessed quickly without having to type in the address. You can start on any WWW page in any site and follow links leading to other pages in other sites.

4   A search engine is a program designed to sift through huge quantities of data to find specific items. It must first be given specific instructions about what to look for. The more precise the instructions, the better the result of the search is likely to be. A search engine will normally request key words to describe what a user is looking for and there are several ways of keying in instructions to guide the search engine. These include use of lower or upper case letters, specific word orders, quotation marks, brackets, plus and minus signs and the * symbol, which acts as a wild card that can stand for any character or set of characters. Some advanced searches use the words AND, OR or AND NOT to narrow down choices.

5   The term protocols refers to international standards that have been developed to govern the way data is transferred over the Internet. The aim is to improve speed and reliability of data transfer. Transmission Control Protocol breaks data up into manageable chunks or packets that bear the address they are being sent to. Internet Protocol routes the packets from machine to machine, and TCP then puts data back together in the correct order so that it can be used. The protocols are supplied in the form of specialised software, written to suit the working of the Internet.

6   The user must have the appropriate software to use email. You also need to have an email account, which is usually supplied by the Internet Service Provider. You can then have an email address which is unique to you. You need to know the email address of the person you are writing to, also.

The software allows messages to be written and addressed. It also displays messages received, and normally offers address book and diary functions. Costs can be minimised by preparing and writing messages off-line and logging on only to send and receive messages.

When an outgoing message is finished, it is sent to an Outbox ready for transmission. The same message can be copied to many different people by adding their email addresses to the address box. When you log on, communications software and the modem connect to the ISP's file server. By instructing the system to 'send & receive' any messages in the Outbox will be transmitted, while any incoming messages will be downloaded from the ISP and will go into an Inbox.

7   Email provides a quick way of sending messages all around the world. People are often happy to take a

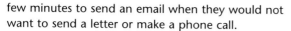

few minutes to send an email when they would not want to send a letter or make a phone call.

The email can be printed, so it could provide valuable proof that a person has agreed to something.

The same message can be sent to many recipients at the same time.

Documents prepared in many types of software can be attached to emails and sent with them.

Users of email can join mailing lists covering specific topics. These give interested people a chance to get together and talk about a subject by email. Some people can discuss problems by email that they cannot express any other way.

The World Wide Web provides a vast source of information and can provide valuable information for research of all kinds.

The results of research can be published immediately on the Web so that information available is always up-to-date.

8   All data is stored in files with file names. Within each file, data is divided into records. A record may contain just one piece of data. In this case it is said to have a single field. A field holds just one piece of data. For example, in a contact list, a person's telephone number might be stored in one field containing the right number of characters.

A record may contain many pieces of related data items, in many fields. For example, a company may store information about each employee in a single record. Each record will consist of a number of fields, one for the name of the employee, one for the National Insurance number, one for the street address, and so on.

A key field is used to describe a field that is unique to a particular record and that can therefore be used to search a file to locate the record quickly. For example, each employee in a large company may be given a unique employee number. Using the number as the key field, the employee's record can easily be found in the company's database.

9   Telecommunications and networks link computers of all kinds all over the world. It is common for people working at terminals either at home or in offices to be linked electronically to other terminals located far away, often via a central computer that acts as the controller. Internet links, telephones, faxes and other specialised electronic equipment make this possible.

Terminals can be either dumb terminals, just a screen and a keyboard, or smart terminals – a screen, keyboard and processor with some backing store. The telecommunications link can be a telephone line, microwave link or radio link.

Chapter 5 *Designing systems*

1   The analysis stage involves finding out exactly what a new system is required to do. A good starting point

for analysis is therefore to examine the existing system – how it works, what improvements are needed and what future developments may be needed.

The new system is then designed. It will often be broken up into separate blocks so that designers can concentrate on these in turn, and particular attention is paid in each case to the design of the human user interface.

A new system is thoroughly tested before it is put into use, to make sure that it can perform all the tasks it is required to perform, and to see what happens if incorrect data is input. As the system is installed, testing continues, and will be carried out throughout the life of the system.

The implementation stage occurs when the system is actually installed and put into use. This is often done in stages, with the most important parts of the system being put into action first.

Documentation is the production of manuals or guidance for those who will work with the system. Technical documentation is produced for the engineers who will maintain and test the system, and user documentation for the people who will use it for the tasks for which it was designed.

Evaluation will be carried out when the system is fully installed and running. Its performance will be checked against the initial design criteria, to see if it meets all the requirements. Evaluation will continue at intervals throughout the life of the system.

The system will require maintenance to keep it running properly. There are three types of maintenance – corrective maintenance fixes faults and breakdowns, adaptive maintenance changes the system to suit changed requirements, and perfective maintenance improves the system beyond its original capability.

2   One method is to observe it being used. This will take some time and should show the conditions under which the system is used. It may bring attention to points that users of the system might not mention themselves.

People who use the system, at all levels, can be interviewed. They should be asked what they think is good or bad about the system.

Questionnaires can be useful where a lot of people use a system. However, it is important to think carefully about the kind of questions to ask. Questionnaires do give people time to think about what they want to say, and they may be more willing to criticise a system in writing than they would be in front of others.

Finally, it is useful to describe the existing system. This description may take the form of a diagram showing the flow of data through the system.

3   It is important that the designer takes care with use of both colour and sound. Both can help users, or

distract or annoy them. Use of flashing symbols must also be carefully judged for the same reasons. The location of items on the screen is important because users are believed to see the upper half of screens better than the lower areas. Movement from screen to screen must be consistent and straightforward, and users will also need a consistent way of indicating choices that they have to make. The designer must also use language that is appropriate for the likely users of the system.

Chapter 6 *Security*

1 Electronic fraud is one example. This involves exploiting the weaknesses of information systems to commit deceptive acts for financial gain, e.g. setting up false suppliers in a company's database and making payments to them. Credit card fraud is a second example and involves stealing people's credit cards and using them illegally.

2 The Data Protection Act applies to both computer-held and manual records and is applicable within the European economic area. Its aim is to control technological ability to transmit personal data, and to protect the individual's right to privacy. It states that personal data must be processed fairly and lawfully, and within the rights of the individual. Any data held must be accurate and up-to-date, and must be kept secure.

3 1; **4** 4; **5** 1; **6** 2.

Chapter 7 *Information systems in society*

1 Advantages: Improved productivity; improved competitiveness as a result of reduced labour costs. Disadvantages: Reduction in number of people employed; high training costs.

2 In service industries, such as shops, hotels, leisure and catering.

3 In the Accounts department, Sales department, Technical department and warehouse.

4 To maintain stock level and control, and in customer accounts.

Chapter 8 *Health and safety*

1 When used by drivers of moving vehicles, the greatest risk posed by mobile telephones and communications systems is that of distracting the driver from what is happening on the road ahead.

Use of mobile telephones is also associated with neck strain and headaches and, more seriously, some research indicates that the radiation emitted by mobile telephones may cause brain tumours.

2 Employers are required to provide office equipment that meets defined standards. The equipment should be inspected. Jobs should be designed so that they do not require long hours without a break in front of monitors. Employees should be trained in computer use, and are entitled to eye tests paid for by the employer. Standards also apply to lighting and noise levels, and employers should provide software that is appropriate to users' needs.

3 Ideally, lighting should be provided by covered fluorescent tubes that will not cause glare. Natural fibre floor coverings should be used. Adjustable blinds should be fitted to windows. Cables, if not under the floor, should be out of the way so people do not trip on them. Plenty of power sockets should be provided, to avoid overloading.

Centre number	
Candidate number	
Surname and initials	

 **Examining Group**

General Certificate of Secondary Education

ICT
Higher Tier

Time: one hour

Instructions to candidates

Use blue or black ink or ball-point pen.

Write your name in the box above.

Write your Centre number and the Candidate number in the boxes above.

Answer all questions in the spaces given.

Show all stages of your calculations.

Do not show rough work on this question paper.

Cross through any work you do not want marked.

Information for candidates

The maximum mark for this paper is 120.

The number of marks is given in brackets **[ ]** at the end of each question or part question.

You are reminded of the need for good English and clear presentation of your answers.

For Examiner's use only	
1	
2	
3	
4	
5	
6	
7	
8	
9	
10	
11	
12	
13	
14	
15	
16	
17	
18	
19	
20	
21	
22	
23	
24	
25	
26	
27	
28	
29	
30	
Total	

EDUCATIONAL

Section A

Multiple choice questions

1 Which of the following devices is suitable for connecting a workstation to a local area network (LAN)?

- **a)** modem ☐
- **b)** network interface card ☐
- **c)** hub ☐
- **d)** switch ☐ **[1]**

2 Which part of a computer's hardware is responsible for carrying out a program's instructions?

- **a)** processor ☐
- **b)** RAM ☐
- **c)** hard disk ☐
- **d)** ROM ☐ **[1]**

3 How much data can be stored in one memory location in RAM?

- **a)** 1 bit ☐
- **b)** 1 byte ☐
- **c)** 1 kilobyte ☐
- **d)** 1 megabyte ☐ **[1]**

4 Which of these is an input device?

- **a)** disk ☐
- **b)** monitor ☐
- **c)** motor ☐
- **d)** sensor ☐ **[1]**

5 The ability of a computer to apparently run more than one program at the same time is called:

- **a)** multi-programming ☐
- **b)** multi-tasking ☐
- **c)** multi-access ☐
- **d)** multi-user ☐ **[1]**

6 Validation is carried out when data is:

- **a)** input ☐
- **b)** stored ☐
- **c)** processed ☐
- **d)** copied ☐ **[1]**

7 One method of validating a number such as a bar code number is to perform a calculation to produce an extra character. This character appears at the end of the original number. This method of validation involves:

- **a)** a parity check ☐
- **b)** a hash total ☐
- **c)** a checksum ☐
- **d)** a check digit ☐ **[1]**

8 When a program is about to be run, which of these could be true? The program is copied:

- **a)** from RAM to disk ☐
- **b)** from RAM to ROM ☐
- **c)** from a storage device to RAM ☐
- **d)** from RAM to the processor ☐ **[1]**

9 A number has to be entered into a database. It is first checked by the database software to make sure that it is really a number and not a letter. This is an example of:

- **(a)** verification ☐
- **b)** parity checking ☐
- **c)** format checking ☐
- **d)** validation ☐ **[1]**

10 A word-processed document is produced that forms the basis of many other documents. When a new document of the same type is required, it is loaded and then changed or added to as required.

This basic document is called:

- **a)** a macro ☐
- **b)** a style ☐
- **c)** a template ☐
- **d)** a theme ☐ **[1]**

11 Which of the following file formats is used to store compressed images?

- **a)** jpeg ☐
- **b)** pdf ☐
- **c)** rtf ☐
- **d)** csv ☐ **[1]**

160

12 A travel agent makes a holiday booking for a customer. The booking is stored in a database table. Which of the following would be a suitable key field for the holiday that has been booked?

a) destination country ❑

b) holiday catalogue number ❑

c) customer name ❑

d) booking reference number ❑ **[1]**

13 An operating system might be responsible for:

a) totalling a column of numbers ❑

b) controlling traffic light timings ❑

c) allocating memory to a program ❑

d) activating a bell in a burglar alarm ❑ **[1]**

14 A program compares two numbers to find which is greater.
This action is carried out in:

a) the central processing unit ❑

b) RAM ❑

c) ROM ❑

d) the control unit ❑ **[1]**

15 The software used to allow a computer to communicate with a peripheral such as a printer is called:

a) an application ❑

b) a driver ❑

c) a utility ❑

d) a protocol ❑ **[1]**

16 Which of these methods of data input is commonly used to read account numbers on cheques?

a) OMR ❑

b) OCR ❑

c) bar codes ❑

d) MICR ❑ **[1]**

17 Which of the following is a peripheral device?

a) motherboard ❑

b) disk controller ❑

c) temperature sensor ❑

d) RAM ❑ **[1]**

18 Which of these is a correct sequence of memory sizes, starting with the smallest and ending with the biggest?

smallest/middle/largest

a) 1 megabyte/2048 kilobytes/ 1 gigabyte ❑

b) 2048 kilobytes/1 megabyte/ 1 gigabyte ❑

c) 1 gigabyte/2048 kilobytes/ 1 megabyte ❑

d) 1 gigabyte/1 megabyte/ 2048 kilobytes ❑ **[1]**

19 A new computer system is being planned. It will store a lot of data in data tables. Decisions have to be made about what data goes into each table. During which stage are these decisions made?

a) investigation ❑

b) analysis ❑

c) design ❑

d) implementation ❑ **[1]**

20 A computer system is used to keep an aircraft at a steady altitude throughout a flight. The mode of operation that would be needed for this purpose is:

a) batch processing ❑

b) transaction processing ❑

c) interactive processing ❑

d) real-time processing ❑ **[1]**

21 The parents of each student in a school are to be sent an end of term report. The format of the report is the same for everyone, but the remarks and test scores vary. Mail merge is to be used.

State the **two** files that are necessary to produce the reports.

....

.... **[2]**

22 Here is a list of parts that might be found in a burglar alarm system.
For each component part, state whether it is an input or an output device.

Part	Input or output
bell	
infra-red detector	
flashing light	
pressure pad	
key pad on control unit	

[5]

23 Many schools use an OMR system to record student attendances.

a) Explain the meaning of OMR.

....

.... **[2]**

b) Explain how data is collected and entered into the school's computer system using an OMR system.

....

.... **[2]**

c) State **two** other situations where OMR data entry might be appropriate.

....

.... **[2]**

d) Explain **one** technical problem that may occur when using an OMR system.

....

.... **[2]**

24 A supermarket changes from an EPOS system to an EFTPOS system.

a) Explain the difference between these two systems.

....

.... **[2]**

b) State **two** advantages of an EFTPOS system compared with an EPOS system to a customer.

....

.... **[2]**

c) State **two** advantages of an EFTPOS system compared with an EPOS system to the supermarket.

....

.... **[2]**

25 The supermarket introduces a loyalty card scheme. The customers can collect points whenever they shop. The points can be used to get money off future purchases or may be used in various special offers.

Before customers can use the loyalty card scheme, they have to fill in a form with many personal details.

a) State **two** ways that the supermarket can benefit from the introduction of a loyalty card scheme.

....

.... **[2]**

b) State **three** data items that the supermarket would need to collect on the application form.

....

....

.... **[3]**

c) Give **two** reasons why some customers might not want to provide personal details.

....

.... **[2]**

d) The supermarket tries to reassure customers who fill in the form by saying that there is a law that protects customers in this sort of situation.

State what this law is.

.... **[1]**

(e) State any **three** aspects of this law that would reassure customers who gave their personal details.

....

....

.... **[3]**

26 A school has the details of all its students and staff on a large database.
One of the secretaries notices that some data on a student has been changed.
The school's systems manager thinks that this has been caused by hacking.

a) Explain what is meant by hacking.

....

.... **[2]**

b) Explain **two** ways that the systems manager might be able to reduce the likelihood of hacking.

....

....

....

.... **[4]**

c) On investigation, it is found that several files have been altered since the day before. There could be more that nobody has seen yet. Describe what the systems manager should do to cure the problems caused by the altered files.

....

....

....

.... **[2]**

d) The systems manager also tries to protect data against viruses.

Explain what a computer virus is.

....

.... **[2]**

(e) Explain **two** ways that problems from computer viruses can be avoided.

....

....

....

.... **[4]**

27 Walker & Co is opening a new sports shop. The manager wants to advertise the launch of the new shop in the local area.

One of the advertising methods that has been considered is to produce a leaflet. The manager uses a computer to produce this leaflet, using desk top publishing, word processing and graphics capture software.

a) Explain how each of these software packages would be used in producing the leaflet.

    i) DTP

    ....

    .... **[2]**

    ii) Word processing

    ....

    .... **[2]**

    iii) Graphics capture software

    ....

    .... **[2]**

b) Walker & Co also want to set up a website to advertise the new shop. Describe **two** advantages of using a website to promote the business.

....

.... **[2]**

c) Walker & Co employ a web designer, Debra, to produce the website. She has to use HTML code. Explain what is meant by HTML code.

....

....

.... **[3]**

d) State **two** types of software that can be used to produce HTML code.

....

.... **[2]**

e) State the type of software that is needed to display pages created in HTML code.

.... **[1]**

f) The manager of the sports shop wants to put lots of pictures on the website. Debra explains that until more of the public has access to broadband Internet facilities, the number of pictures should be kept to a minimum.

Explain why Debra thinks that the number of pictures should be kept small.

....

.... **[2]**

g) **(i)** Explain what is meant by **broadband**.

....

.... **[2]**

(ii) Explain why widespread broadband availability could make a difference to the amount of graphics that web designers use on web pages.

....

.... **[2]**

28 A company has been using an application to process orders for many years. The application manages a large database. The company decides that the application needs to be upgraded.

a) State **four** reasons why an application might need to be upgraded.

....

....

....

.... **[4]**

b) The company employs a systems analyst to investigate what will have to be done in the new application. List **three** ways that the system analyst could find out what is needed in the new system.

....

....

.... **[3]**

c) The system is then designed. State **two** items that need to be designed in the new software package.

....

.... **[2]**

d) Each order is given an order number. Order numbers are integers between 1 and 100 000. The system must not allow operators to enter incorrect order numbers. This is tested using normal, extreme and unusual data.

State one item of test data that is normal, one that is extreme and one that is unusual. Explain why you have chosen these.

Normal: ....

....

Extreme: ....

....

Unusual: ....

.... **[6]**

e) User documentation is produced for the finished application.

List **three** sections that you would expect to find in this application's user documentation.

....

....

.... **[3]**

29 The following flow chart shows part of a computer-controlled system. It counts the cars entering a car park and, if the car park is not full, it allows them to enter.

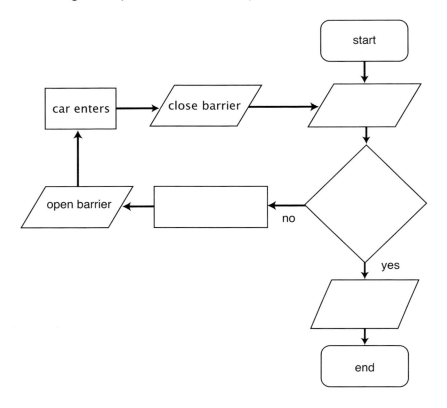

Here are some of the stages that need to be placed into the flow chart. Copy them into the correct boxes.

no_cars=max

sign='CAR PARK FULL'

car detected

no_cars=no_cars+1

[4]

30 Komal invests some of her money in the stock market. She has bought shares in seven companies. She keeps details of how well the share prices are doing month by month in a spreadsheet. The figures for the first six months of the year are shown below.

	A	B	C	D	E	F	G	H	I	J	K
1					My Share Portfolio						
2				Company performance by month							
3	Name of company	January	February	March	April	May	June	Average price	Max price	Min price	
4	Great Northern Hotels	503.3	553.2	556.7	408.9	443.4	643.3	518.1333333	643.3	408.9	
5	Cedric's Travel	123.4	145.8	125.4	113.4	102.3	118.4	121.45	145.8	102.3	
6	Capital and Counties Bank	437.6	453.8	468.7	437.3	489.4	490.1	462.8166667	490.1	437.3	
7	United Power	235.6	345.6	255.6	221.4	204.5	183.4	241.0166667	345.6	183.4	
8	AB Computers	993.4	867.3	453.4	114.5	115.5	164.5	451.4333333	993.4	114.5	
9	Yukon Oil	355.6	368.7	327.6	316.5	369.6	362.2	350.0333333	369.6	316.5	
10	Granada Media	132.6	145.6	146.6	146.6	158.6	142.4	145.4	158.6	132.6	

a) State the address of a cell that contains text data.

.... **[1]**

b) State the addresses of a range of cells that has been merged.

.... **[1]**

c) Cell J4 contains a function.

i) Explain what a spreadsheet function is.

....

.... **[2]**

ii) State the function that would be present in cell J4.

.... **[2]**

iii) State the function that would be present in cell H10.

.... **[2]**

iv) The data displayed in cells H4 to H10 are not formatted sensibly. Explain the steps you would need to take to make the display in these cells fit in with the rest of the sheet.

....

....

....

.... **[4]**

Answers: GCSE ICT paper

General tips

● You do not need to write a lot to gain the marks in ICT examinations. The marks are awarded for giving the correct points, as you will see in the following mark scheme.

● There is space allocated for you to write your answers. You will never need to write more than will fit into the space. Often there is more space than you need.

● Be on the lookout for questions that require a fact plus an explanation. You will get a clue that a question is like this if there are two marks allocated or if the question says 'describe' or 'explain'. You only need to put one word or idea down per point when the question says 'state' or 'list'.

● Beware of answering questions with generally unhelpful remarks like something is *easier*, *quicker*, etc. You will always need to say *what* is easier or quicker.

● You will generally have more time than you need so there is no need to rush.

● Try to use IT terminology where appropriate, rather than just giving a 'general knowledge' type of response.

● If you are asked for a type of software that is suitable for some purpose, avoid using brand names. Some boards automatically reject such answers. Use the correct *generic* term such as *word processor*, *DTP*, *web browser*, *spreadsheet* and *database management software*.

● Take care with your handwriting. Examiners always see some answers that just cannot be read. Examiners cannot award marks if they cannot understand what you have written.

Mark scheme

Note: In the case of the longer questions, there may be acceptable responses that differ slightly from the answers given here. In a real GCSE exam, the examiners will make allowances for correct but unexpected answers.
This mark scheme contains some examiner's tips as well as the acceptable answers that an examiner would be asked to look for.

Section A

Multiple choice questions

Question	Answer	Mark
1	b	1
2	a	1
3	b	1
4	d	1
5	b	1
6	a	1
7	d	1
8	c	1
9	d	1
10	c	1
11	a	1
12	d	1
13	c	1
14	a	1
15	b	1
16	d	1
17	c	1
18	a	1
19	c	1
20	d	1

Section B

21

Document: the report format/template
Database or spreadsheet: the student
data/comments/test scores   **2**

22

Examiner's tip

There are usually questions on input, storage and output
devices. Be ready for less obvious examples that you have
to think about.

Part	Input or output
bell	output
infra-red detector	input
flashing light	output
pressure pad	input
key pad on control unit	input

5

23

Examiner's tip

Questions on standard automated data capture are common.
Be aware of how they work, be ready with examples of
their use and know their advantages and drawbacks.

a   *Any two*:
Optical Mark Recognition (or Reading)
a system for reading pen or pencil marks
on paper
values decoded according to position
on paper   **2**

b   *Any two*:
specially printed form used
marks made with pen or pencil
read by reading machine
data passed to computer   **2**

c   *Any two*:
selection of lottery numbers
answering multiple choice exams
entering marks scored in exam
other suitable scenario   **2**

d   *Any of these problems: 2 marks – 1 for
problem; 1 for explanation*:
paper gets crumpled; won't enter
reading machine
marks misaligned; wrong data read or mis-read
wrong batch total or no batch total entered;
wrong amount of data read   **2**

24

Examiner's tip

IT in the 'real world' is a common exam scenario. The
scenarios will probably be chosen to be familiar to you, so
expect supermarkets, doctors' surgeries, banks, garages, etc.
Stock control and cashless transactions are often examined.

a   EPOS is concerned with scanning goods at
checkout
EFTPOS additionally has electronic **payment**
method   **2**

b   *Any two*:
no need to carry cash
availability of cashback service
can use credit card to defer payment   **2**

c   *Any two*:
less cash on hand – security issue
customer satisfaction
customers might spend more (not restricted by
amount of cash they have)   **2**

25

Examiner's tip

The theme of data privacy is often in the exam. Make sure
you know the main provisions of the Data Protection Act
and why it is needed.

a   *Any two*:
more customers/customers likely to return
can collect shopping data on customers
more targeted promotions/advertising   **2**

b   name
address
post code/telephone/email address (*any one*) **3**

Examiner's tip

Other questions such as date of birth or gender may be
asked, but these are not strictly essential.

c   *Any two*:
any comment about invasion of privacy
fear that others will have access to their details
concern about junk mail
incorrect data may be stored   **2**

d   Data Protection Act   **1**

e   *Any three*:
can check to see that details are correct
data cannot be passed to anyone else
without permission
data must be kept secure
data must be accurate   **3**

26

Examiner's tip
Be aware of issues of security. This covers both protection of data against criminal activity and also against accidents. You should know a wide variety of potential problems and how they can be dealt with.

a accessing someone else's computer files without their permission **2**

b *Any two processes plus explanation*:
set access rights: restricts who can view which files;
arrange for passwords to be changed regularly: reduces likelihood of passwords being discovered;
insist on effective passwords such as must contain a number: less easy for hacker to guess;
procedures such as not leaving of passwords on display: prevents visitors seeing passwords;
firewall: control over external access;
procedures such as log out when not at computer; prevent passers-by accessing system **4**

c *Any two*:
restore any files
updated during that period
from backup **2**

d *Any two*:
a computer program
designed to copy itself
may cause damage **2**

e *Any two methods plus explanations*:
don't open emails from unknown sources; they may contain a virus/macro virus
don't download software from the Internet; source may be untrustworthy/viruses often attached to program files
don't bring in disks from home; may have been contaminated
install scanning software; catches viruses as they appear
update scanning software; new viruses appearing all the time
no floppy drive on workstations; avoid problems of files introduced on floppies
sanctions against those who do not follow procedures; discourage careless behaviour **4**

27

Examiner's tip
The main types of 'generic' software are often examined. Modern software is powerful and versatile. However, you should be aware of exactly what each type is best used for. For example, document work can be carried out by word processing or DTP software, but strictly speaking, DTP is best for doing layouts and word processing for text origination. Try to keep up to date with the hardware and software that is increasingly being used by ordinary individuals as well as by businesses.

a i set out page layouts
bring together text and graphics **2**

ii *Any two*:
produce the text
edit the text
formatting features such as fonts **2**

iii *Any two*:
collect images from digital camera
collect images from scanner
manipulate images **2**

b *Any two*:
widespread/worldwide coverage
easily updated
can combine with ebusiness
provide a means of contact
can be made interactive – multimedia – more interesting than paper-based advertising **2**

c *Any three*:
Hypertext markup language
set of codes/tags
that describe how to display the page
interpreted by browser **3**

d

Examiner's tip
Because of the ever increasing extent and importance of the Internet, there will always be questions to do with this. You are expected to know a reasonable amount about how to produce websites as well as look at them. If you have created your own website, preferably not just using an on-line facility, you will be well placed to handle questions of this sort. Be aware that a plain text editor is a perfectly good way of writing HTML code – as long as you know what you are doing!

Any two:
text editor
web authoring package
any part of modern office software such as

172

word processor, spreadsheet, presentation software, DTP, some database packages **2**

e browser
don't allow brand names **1**

f

Examiner's tip
Issues of bandwidth are common on exam papers these days. You should thoroughly understand what the consequences of increasing bandwidth are.

Any two:
pictures are often large files
slow to download
people may get bored and leave site **2**

g **i** Internet access
with high rate of data transfer **2**

ii can use more/bigger graphics files
as more people can download
them quickly **2**

28

Examiner's tip
Be ready for questions on the system life cycle. You need to know what happens when. This type of question ought to be easy for you if you have done your coursework carefully and thoroughly!

a *Any four*:
too slow
difficult to use
can't cope with the amount of data
new working practices
new legislation
new operating system
new hardware **4**

b *Any three*:
interview
questionnaire
observation
discussion/focus groups **3**

c *Any two*:
interface
data tables
database structure
programmed modules
queries
reports **2**

d Normal: any whole number between 2 and 99 999; these are numbers that fall within the correct range
Extreme: 1 or 100,000; these are numbers at the boundary of the permitted range but still acceptable
Unusual: any other data item such as −1, 100,001, 3.5. z; items that are not permissible (too big, too small, not whole numbers, not numbers)
For each item, 1 mark for the data plus 1 mark for an explanation **6**

e *Any three*:
installation
troubleshooting
how to use it/enter data/amend data/delete data
walk through/tutorial
backing up **3**

29

Examiner's tip
Flow charts are having a bit of a come back lately. You must be very clearly aware of the differences between system flow charts (showing data flow through a whole computer system) and program flow charts (like this one), which show the steps to solve a problem. Be careful – the shapes used are not quite the same in the two types of flow chart.

One mark per correct box

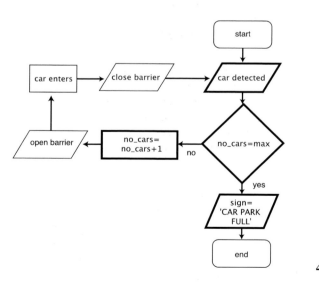

4

30

Examiner's tip

Spreadsheet questions are common. You will either have to make a few comments and identify what is going on in a spreadsheet that you are given or you may be asked to design the layout of a spreadsheet for a particular purpose.

a		any one cell from A3 to A10 or B1 to G1, B2 to G2, B3 to J3	1
b		*Either point*: B1 to G1 B2 to G2	1
c	i	preset/pre-programmed formula/expression/mathematical relationship/set of instructions	2
	ii	=MIN(B4:G4) *1 mark for MIN, 1 mark for correct range of cells*	2
	iii	=AVERAGE(B10:G10) *1 mark for AVERAGE, 1 mark for correct range of cells*	2

Examiner's tip

The correct result could be produced by making up your own formula but that won't do here as the question specifically asks for a **function**.

| | iv | *Any four*:
highlight/select range
select format/cells
select number
set decimal places = 2 | 4 |

Total 120 marks

Grade predictor

These grade boundaries are only a rough indication. The position of the boundaries is not the same for each exam board, nor is it the same each year. The boundaries are arrived at after a consideration of the difficulty of the particular paper.

Mark range	Grade
0–18	U
19–24	G
25–33	F
34–42	E
43–53	D
54–66	C
67–78	B
79–90	A
90–120	A*

The importance of coursework

It is also extremely important to realise that the exam is only 40% of your final assessment. The remaining 60% will already be determined by your coursework. This is an unusually high percentage for a GCSE exam. If you have produced really good quality coursework, you could already have a grade C before you even take the exam.

Index

access time 36, 37
actuators 34
adaptive maintenance 116
algorithms 113
ALU see arithmetic and logic unit
analogue signals 11–12, 23
    modems 91, 92
applications software 38, 46, 53–72
arithmetic and logic unit (ALU) 18
ASCII 103
assembly language 52
automatic dialling 92

backing storage 35, 36–40
    LANs 85
    security 122, 123, 127
bad sectors 49
bandwidth 93
bar codes 24
barcode readers 24
batch files 51
batch processing 83
baud 91
binary code 12–13, 51, 128
bit maps 64–5
bits 12
bits per second 91
blocks 39–40
bookmarks 97
boot program 36
bubble-jet printers see ink-jet
buffers 70
bus topology see line topology
business graphics programs 65
buzzers 34
bytes 12

cable modems 92
cables
    health and safety 148–9, 151
    modems 91
    networks 86, 87, 89
CAD see Computer Aided Design
cameras, digital 23–4, 64
CD-R 38–9
CD-ROMs 36, 38–9, 132
CD-RW 38–9, 124
central controllers 89
central processing unit (CPU) 18
    hard disks 37
    memory 35–6
check digits 129
clients, networks 89–90
clip art 38, 67
codes 102–3
    see also binary code
    encryption 126–7
    system design 113
colour
    printers 32
    screens 29
    system design 112
command-driven interface 46, 47
communication 82
compact disks 38
compilers 52
Computer Aided Design (CAD) 22, 64, 66, 69
Computer Misuse Act 1990 134
concept keyboards 19–20
control devices 34
control software 69–71
control systems
    data logging 130
    real-time processing 83
control units 18
Copyright, Designs and Patents Act 1989 135
corrective maintenance 116

CPU see central processing unit
credit card fraud 134

data
    definition 9
    entering 102–3
    feedback 11
    input peripherals 19–28
    loss 124–5, 151
    misuse 133–6, 140
    modems 91
    preparation 113
    quality 128–33
    representation of 11–13
    security 121–5, 126–7, 144–5
    storage 10, 35–40, 49
data logging 69–70, 130
Data Protection Act 1998 135–6
database management systems (DBMs) 56
databases
    data protection 135
    LANs 85
    mail-order companies 142–4
    software 53–4, 55–60
DBMs see database management systems
dedicated file server 84, 86
designing systems 109–20
desk top publishing (DTP) 62–3
device drivers 50
digital cameras 23–4, 64
digital networks 92
digital signals 11–13
    modems 91, 92
digital versatile disks (DVD) 40, 132
direct access storage 39
direct implementation 114
disk directory 51
documentation 115–16
dot matrix printers 30, 31
downloading 91
drawing software 65
DTP see desk top publishing
dumb terminals 82
dust 122
DVD see digital versatile disks

EFTPOS see electronic fund transfer point of sale
electronic fraud 133–4
electronic fund transfer point of sale (EFTPOS) terminals 27
electronic point of sale (EPOS) terminals 27
email 10, 100–1
    encryption 127
    LANs 85, 86
    society 140
embedded systems 18
encoding 102
encryption 126–7
EPOS see electronic point of sale
evaluation 116
external communications links 91–3
eye strain 148, 149–50

fax machines 82, 92
feasibility reports 110–11
feedback 9, 11, 70
fields 102–3
file names 102
file servers 89
files 102, 113
flat file databases 56
flat screens 30
flexible membrane 19–20
floor turtles 71
floppy disks 36, 37–8, 124
formatting 37

fraud 133–4
function keys 20
furniture 151

general purpose packages 54
golf ball printers 31
graphical user interface (GUI) 46, 47–8
graphics
    input peripherals 23–4
    output devices 31–2, 33–4, 131–2
    software 64–6
    storage 38
graphics digitisers 22
GUI see graphical user interface

hacking 125, 134
hard disks 36, 37
hardware 16–45
    networks 87
    security 122–3
    system design 113, 114
HCI see human computer interface
health and safety 148–53
hierarchical networks 87, 89
high-level language 52
home pages 97
HTML see Hyper Text Markup Language
http see Hypertext Transfer Protocol
human computer interface (HCI) 46–8
Hyper Text Markup Language (HTML) 67, 97
hypertext databases 57
Hypertext Transfer Protocol (http) 97

IAS see immediate access store
ID 126
immediate access store (IAS) 18
impact printers 31
implementation 114–15
in-car communications systems 150
information
    definition 9
    output 29–35, 130–2
Information Superhighway 9–10
information systems 9–15
    operating environment 46
    in society 139–47
infra-red technology 24
ink-jet printers 30, 31, 32–3
input peripherals 10, 19–28
inputs 9
    definition 10
    diagrams 17
    operating system 49
    system design 113
Integrated Services Digital Network (ISDN) 92–3
integrated software 53–4
interfaces 46–8, 70, 112
interlacing 30
Internet 94–9
    definition 9–10
    quality of data 129
    telecommunications 82
    WANs 86
Internet Protocol (IP) address 96
Internet Service Provider (ISP) 94–5, 96
interpreters 52
Intranets 85
IP see Internet Protocol
ISDN see Integrated Services Digital Network
ISP see Internet Service Provider

joysticks 21–2

key fields 103
keyboards 19–21
kilobyte 13

languages 51–2
LANs *see* Local Area Networks
laser printers 30, 31–2
light pens 22
lights, control devices 34
line (bus) topology 85, 87, 88
LINUX 48
liquid crystal displays 29
Local Area Networks (LANs) 84, 85–6
locations 13, 36
LOGO 71
low-level languages 52

machine code 51, 52
macro programs 55
magnetic ink character recognition (MICR) 26
magnetic storage media 37
magnetic strips 26
magnetic tape 39–40
mail merging 61
mail-order companies 142–5
main store memory 35–6
main-frame computers 18
maintenance 116–17
megabyte 13
memory
    see also storage
    operating system 48–9
    storage devices 35–40
memory cards 23
menu-driven interface 46, 47
mice 21
MICR *see* magnetic ink character recognition
micro-chips 17
micro-computer systems 17
microphones 28
Microsoft Windows 48
MIDI *see* musical instrument digital interface
mobile telephones 17, 150
modelling software 68–9
modems 91–2, 94
modes 49
monitors 29–30
monochrome 29
motherboard 36, 87
motors, control devices 34
mouse *see* mice
multi-processor modes 49
multi-tasking mode 49
multi-user mode 49
multimedia output 132
multimedia software 34
musical instrument digital interface (MIDI) 28

network cards 87
networks 82–108
    definition 84
    digital 92
    security 125
    system design 113
nodes 87–9, 94
non-impact printers 31–3
non-volatile memory 36

OCR *see* optical character recognition
OMR *see* optical mark readers
operating environment 46–53
operating system 48–53
    back-ups 127
    networks 87
    ROM 36
optical character recognition (OCR) 23, 25
optical disks 38–9
optical mark readers (OMR) 25
output peripherals 29–35
outputs 9
    definition 11
    diagrams 17
    operating system 49
    presentation 130–2
    system design 112

packets 95–6
painting software 65
paper 30, 33, 140

parallel ports 92
parallel running 115
passwords 85, 86, 124, 126
PDAs *see* personal digital assistants
perfective maintenance 117
peripherals 17
    see also input peripherals; output peripherals
personal digital assistants (PDAs) 17
personal information 133, 135–6
phased implementation 115
pixels 30
plotters 33–4
point of presence (PoP) 94
point and touch methods 19–20, 21
PoP *see* point of presence
presentation software 62–3
print servers 89–90
printed output 131
printers 30–3
    device drivers 50
    memory 36
    networks 85, 86, 90
    parallel ports 92
privacy 121, 135–6
processing 9, 11
programming languages 51–2
programs *see* software
protocols 95–6
pseudocodes 113

radiation 150
RAM *see* random access memory
random access memory (RAM) 35–6
read-only memory (ROM) 35–6
read/write heads 37
real-time processing 83
record-structured databases 58
records 102
reel-to-reel tape 39
relational databases 56–7, 142–4
remote sensors 27, 70
repetitive strain injury (RSI) 149
reproduction 150
requirement specification 111
resolution 30
ring topology 86, 87, 88
robots, control devices 34
ROM *see* read-only memory
RSI *see* repetitive strain injury

safety *see* health and safety; security
scanners 23, 25, 30
screen output 131–2
screens 29–30
    health and safety 148, 149–50, 151
search engines 97–9
search path 51
security 121–38
    LANs 86
    mail-order companies 144–5
sensors 27, 69–70
serial access storage 39
serial ports 92
servers 89
shareware 124
shift key 20
simulation software 68–9
single program mode 49
smart terminals 82
software 46–80
    email 100
    LANs 85
    laws 135
    memory 36
    networks 87, 95–6
    security 123–4
    storage 38
    system design 113, 114
    validation checks 129
sound output 112, 132
speakers 34
speech recognition systems 28
spreadsheets 53–4, 58–60, 68
standard keyboards 20–1
star topology 87, 89
storage 9, 35–40

back-ups 35, 122, 123, 127
    definition 10
    LANs 85
structure diagrams 111
subdirectories 51
subsystems 111
super disks 37, 38
surfing 97, 101
synthesisers 28
system analysis 109–11
system life cycles 109
system security 49
system utility programs 49–50
systems 9–15
    hardware 16–45
    security 121–5
systems software 46

tailor-made software 54
TCP/IP *see* Transmission Control Protocol/Internet Protocol
technical documentation 116
telecommunications 82–3
telecommuting 82
telephone lines 91
telephones 17, 82, 150
televisions 17
templates 55
terminals 82
    email 100
    networks 87
testing 114
text files 103
theft 122–3, 127
time slices 49
time slot 48
topologies 87
touch sensitive pads 21
touch sensitive screens 22
track pads 21
tracker ball 21
transmission capacity 93
Transmission Control Protocol/Internet Protocol (TCP/IP) system 95–6

Uniform Resource Locator (URL) 97
Universal Serial Port (USB) 92
UNIX 48
URL *see* Uniform Resource Locator
USB *see* Universal Serial Port
user documentation 115
user interface 46–8
user names 86

validation checks 129
VDUs *see* visual display units
vector graphics 64
verification checks 128
video, DVDs 40
video conferencing 93
video digitisers 23
virtual reality 132
viruses 86, 101, 123–4, 134
visual display units (VDUs) 29
    health and safety 148, 149–50
voice mail systems 28
voice synthesis 34
volatile memory 36

WANs *see* Wide Area Networks
Web *see* World Wide Web
web browsers 96–7
web design, software 67–8
websites *see* World Wide Web
Wide Area Networks (WANs) 84, 86–7
WIMP environment 47–8
word processing 53–4, 60–2, 103
work
    effect of ICT 140–1
    health and safety 148–53
World Wide Web 94, 96–9, 101
    definition 9–10
    quality of data 129
    society 140

zip disks, security 124
zip drives 38